Guide to Taxidermy

Charles K. Reed

and

Chester A. Reed

Drawings and Photographs of Mounted Specimens
by the Authors and Mr. N. F. Stone

D1571245

Skyhorse Publishing

Publisher's Note: This is a facsimile of *Guide to Taxidermy*, originally published in 1908. This book is intended as an artifact—not as a contemporary guide to taxidermy. The materials, instructions, and techniques described in these pages may not be safe or effective for modern use.

Visit our website at www.skyhorsepublishing.com.

10 9 8 7 6 5 4 3 2 1

Library of Congress Cataloging-in-Publication Data is available on file.

ISBN: 978-1-61608-539-1

Printed in China

PREFACE

The object of this book is to enable the reader to gain complete mastery of the art of taxidermy. We do not believe in the wanton destruction of birds for ornamental purposes, nor do the laws in most states, if properly enforced, allow of such practices. We do believe, however, that at least one person in every community should possess the knowledge to enable him to correctly mount specimens.

Millions of birds are killed yearly in the United States by accidents, such as flying against lighthouses, telegraph wires, or buildings, etc. Practically none of these are saved because there is no one at hand who has the requisite knowledge.

If only a fraction of one per cent. of all the birds killed accidentally, and those shot by sportsmen and thrown away, could be saved and correctly prepared it would be unnecessary to shoot thousands that are now killed every year simply for museum purposes.

We trust that this book may be the means of creating a taxidermist or an enthusiast in every section of the country, and that each one of them will endeavor to persuade sportsmen to save most of the game they kill. You will find that there is pleasure in doing the work for yourself and profit in doing that for others.

In the following pages we give you the results of our thirty-five years' experience in all branches of taxidermy. No trade secrets are held back; everything is laid bare. We have endeavored to omit nothing that would be a help to the student and to avoid the introduction of any hindrances.

We have illustrated every point as fully as possible, and are sure that any faithful reader and worker can in a short time do work equal to that of the best. The text, every drawing and every photograph used in this book is new and made expressly for this work. We wish to give credit to our chief taxidermist, Mr. N. F. Stone, who mounted a large number of the specimens that are pictured; while a young man, he is one of the best that this country has yet produced, a natural-born taxidermist.

We shall be more than pleased if, by our work, others can be produced.

Chas. K. & C. A. Reed.

Worcester, Massachusetts.

May, 1908.

Brown Thrasher
(On a natural twig for museum exhibition.)

TABLE OF CONTENTS

Material Required
Wiring the Legs
Wiring the Tail
Pinning Wings
Putting Eyes in Birds
Finishing the Specimen
Making T Perches
Spreading a Bird's Wings
Long-necked Birds
In Fancy Attitudes
Mounting Collossal Birds
Relaxing Dried Skins
Making a Bird Skin
Cleaning the Feathers
Unusual Forms for Skins
Hanging "Dead Game" Birds

Skinning
Making the Body
Mounting
Skinning Large Animals
Making the Manikin
Exceptional Cases
Covering the Manikin
Putting on the Skin

Myrtle Warblers
Sparrow Hawks

LIST OF ILLUSTRATIONS

Chickadee
Chestnut-collared Lockspur
Golden-fronted Woodpecker. Gilded Flicker
(Some well made skins)

IMPORTANT

Read These Pages Before Doing Any Work

In the following chapters we give the best methods of skinning and mounting the members of several classes of the animal kingdom.

Whatever you are to work on, read the Chapter appertaining to it through before doing any of the work. We ask you to do this because it may cause you to avoid some false move. We have made all instructions as plain as possible, and as nearly as possible in their natural sequence, but the different operations are so closely related to one another that you should know what is coming next before you commence work.

If your specimen is to be mounted, fix upon a certain position before you commence and have that position in mind throughout the work. The illustrations that we give are natural and artistic ones for the different species and you will do well to select some of these for your first models.

Chapter 10 gives the materials and tools that are

often used or needed by taxidermists, where to get them or how to make them. Of course a beginner will need but very few of these, but we have everything arranged in alphabetical order so you can find what you want or anything that may be mentioned in the text. It gives receipts for making solutions used by, or useful for, taxidermists.

Chapter 11 gives the sizes and colors of eyes for a great many birds and animals so you can, at least determine what size eye you wish for any specimen. It also has a plate illustrating the different sizes and styles of eyes. A list of the sizes of wire used for many different specimens will guide you as to what you should have on hand for your work. It also gives the prices that are charged by expert and reputable taxidermists for work of all kinds.

CHAPTER I--Collecting

All taxidermists are not collectors, indeed, most of those who make a business of it, find little time to do any collecting at all.   Yet any work on taxidermy would be far from complete did it not include remarks upon the subject of guns, ammunition and the care of specimens in the field.

For ordinary collecting in your home neighbor hood dress as inconspicuously as possible; wear your usual street clothes.   Do not get a full suit of hunting togs to excite the idle curiosity of everyone you meet.   Most of our collecting is done with a pocket gun and the specimens are brought home in the pocket.

Many of the birds a taxidermist mounts are those found dead or that have killed themselves accidentally.   The collector, however, might hunt for ages without finding a dead bird.   Most of his specimens have to be shot.   Bird lime is absolutely of no use and even if it would catch a bird, the specimen would be in no condition to mount.

Nets and snares of all kinds are of little or no use for catching birds, and their use is prohibited by law most everywhere. So the main and practically only reliance of the collector is his gun.

Kind of Gun

The style and make of gun to use is chiefly a matter of individual taste and pocketbook.

A single-barrel, single shot gun costs the least, but you run the risk of losing a rare specimen by not having another shot in reserve in case of a miss. We have often started up rare birds when shooting at common ones, and without a double-barrel or a repeater it would have been impossible to get them. We would advise that anyone get either a double hammerless gun or a repeater; either of these is excellent and leaves nothing to be desired. Good serviceable guns of either kind can be got for from eighteen to twenty-two dollars.

We would recommend that you purchase as good a gun as you can afford. The bore of the gun is also a matter of your own choice. Either a twelve or sixteen guage are perfect weapons for your purpose. If you expect to do a great deal of collect-

Bald Eagle

ing away from home, we should advise getting the
twelve guage because you can secure ammunition
for it anywhere, whereas some dealers do not carry
smaller guage shells.

The one double-barreled gun will answer for all
the collecting the average taxidermist will do, but
if you are going to make an extensive scientific
collection, it will be far better to also get a small
collecting gun. The best that we know of is made
by the Steven Arms Co. It has a pistol frame,
skeleton stock and either fifteen or eighteen inch
barrel. The best gun of this kind we have ever
seen or owned is one of this make, 32 calibre, 15
in. barrel, chambered for 32 cal. extra long rim-
fire cartridges. The cartridges are bought in
thousand lots, unloaded, but of course primed, for
considerably less than a cent apiece. We load them
with equal bulk of smokeless powder and "dust"
shot; the cartridges are very light and are thrown
away after using. We never carry the stock for
you can shoot perfectly without it; the gun and
twenty-five shells will go in one pocket with no inconvenience whatever.

The question of the right sizes of shot to use is
one that sportsmen often debate spiritedly upon;

there can be but one answer,—use just as small shot as you can and still be sure of getting your bird. We have done considerable shooting ourselves and have handled thousands of specimens killed by others, so we may presume to be pretty well acquainted with this subject. We always use and recommend the use of factory loaded ammunition. Many gun dealers do not carry in stock, cartridges loaded with finer than No. 10 shot, so it may be necessary for you to have them ordered or loaded specially for you, which will be done on an order of 500 shells; or you can buy empty shells and load them yourself.

Since we always carry our collecting gun with us, we never use smaller shot for the double-barrel than No. 10, but if you have no small arm, you will need a large percentage of your shells loaded with either dust or No. 12.

For all small birds up to the size of a jay, we advise the use of the smallest shot you can get.

For larger birds up to a crow, No. 10 is admirably adapted. Crows, hawks, owls, grouse and others of like size are least injured and most certainly obtained with No. 7. Ducks, and in fact nearly all of the largest birds can be secured with No. 4 shot. No 2's are often effective with swans

or geese, but unless you are in a locality where you
can reasonably expect to see them, it is useless to
carry such shells with you.

Of course it goes without saying that any brand
of smokeless powder is far superior to black. It
shoots stronger, makes much less noise and very
little smoke, qualities that would induce anyone to
pay the few cents difference in price for a box of
shells.

Except on rare occasions, a rifle is of little use
for hunting birds. Any bird that you could get
with the rifle, you could probably get with your
shot gun and the chances are usually a hundred to
one in favor of the latter, to say nothing of the
much better condition in which it leaves specimens
for mounting. Still, we believe that everyone
should know how to handle and effectively use a
rifle, and for practice or shooting at squirrels in
most localities no arm is better than a .22 long,
either single shot or repeater, though we much prefer the latter. Probably the best rifle for a careful
and expert collector is the 25-20 repeater. It is a
very powerful small arm, and should not be in
the hands of inexperienced persons for it carries a
long ways; it is very effective for large birds and

most any animals. Smokeless powder is even more
necessary for rifles than shot guns. It does not
readily foul the barrel and where a dozen shots
with a .22, using black powder, would foul the
barrel so as to impair the shooting, hundreds of
them will not appreciably affect it when using
smokeless.

Handling a Gun

A gun in the hands of the careless or ignorant is
a very dangerous weapon; in the hands of careful
or intelligent persons it is no more dangerous than
is a stick. The first instruction to give anyone in
regard to any kind of a firearm is, never to point it
at anyone under any circumstances, loaded or unloaded. And bear in mind it is the supposedly unloaded guns together with a "fool" operator that
are the cause of nearly all accidents.

One summer, I had need of a rifle and asked my
host if he knew where I could get one. Yes, he
did! and immediately went after it. In a few minutes he was back with a Winchester 25-20. Coming
in the door, he dropped the lever just enough to
see that the barrel was empty, put the gun to his
shoulder, aimed playfully at his wife across the
room and pulled the trigger. He had the lever
down and half way back when my hand caught the

Heath Hen

mechanism and stopped him. Just entering the barrel from the magazine was a loaded cartridge. In another instant he would have been an unintentional murderer.

We do not want to harp too much on the dangers of firearms, because, as we said before, in proper hands they are not dangerous, but we do want everyone to use their best precautions in handling them. When carrying a gun through the streets of a city or town always have it unloaded, and carry it with the muzzle pointing towards the ground. The easiest and most convenient positions is shown in sketch. When you are in the woods any convenient method of carrying is permissible, but the muzzle should either point to the sky or the ground. Sketches on this page illustrate some of the least tiring ways of carrying a gun.

Caring for Specimens in the Field

By this we do not mean the skinning or curing of specimens, but simply the keeping of them in suitable condition for such purpose.

We would as soon think of going into the woods or fields without a gun as to go without cotton or paper to wrap our specimens in. On securing any bird, smooth its plumage and, with a small twig, insert a piece of cotton into the throat. This is to prevent blood or juices from injuring the feathers. Also plug up any serious shot wounds from which blood is oozing or apt to come. You can not take too much care in keeping your birds in good condition; you will get better results and much more pleasure out of well-kept birds.

For birds up to the size of a jay, magazine pages make the best wrapping. Roll up a cylinder just a trifle smaller than your specimen, turn one end in and insert your bird head first; then close the other end as shown in sketch opposite. Thus prepared you can put any number of specimens in your game bag or pocket and be sure of their reaching home in fine condition.

Carrying Game

A leather handbag, or a fishing creel, makes the best receptacle for carrying game. It does not allow them to become flattened and mis-shaped and can without inconvenience be carried from the shoulder by a strap.

Killing Wounded Birds

Frequently a bird is "winged" or not killed outright and we wish to put an end to its sufferings immediately. Birds up to the size of an eagle can be most speedily killed by compressing the lungs with the thumb and fingers; this is the most humane way and does no injury to the specimen. The method of holding is shown in sketch opposite. Birds of prey can safely be killed in this manner as they are unable to reach your hand with their talins. Large birds are often killed by plunging a sharp knife under the left wing into the heart; if this is done their mouth and throat must be well filled with cotton and the wound plugged also.

How to Shoot

We take it for granted that everyone knows how to handle a gun, that is, knows how to aim and fire it; still many do not have much success even at sitting objects with a shotgun and even less with a rifle, while they never killed a flying bird except by accident. We think that the reason for most misses is lack of control over the nerves.

I have seen men aim at a sitting bird, sight along the barrel, hesitate, aim again, etc., until the bird in disgust flew away. Do not aim at the bird until you know that you want it, then raise the gun and the instant the front sight touches it pull the trigger. Nothing is gained by waiting, your aim is impaired and frequently the bird goes.

Wing shooting is more difficult and requires a good eye and steady nerves. Here the trouble with most novices is that they cannot control themselves; as soon as the gun points somewhere near the bird they pull the trigger, or even in some cases close the eyes first. If when you fire, the sight is on the head of your bird or a trifle in front, you will be sure to get it. Some ducks, flying broadside to at full speed require "leading" somewhat, but I doubt if the swiftest duck at fifty yards distance can traverse more than three feet before the charge reaches it.

Dogs

Setters, pointers, spaniels and hounds are useful for sportsmen and may be desirable for collectors on some occasions, but few of the latter use them. A collector's "bag" is so varied that a dog is of little use except for retrieving or finding lost birds, and we prefer to pick up our own birds.

How to Find Birds

This is a knowledge that will require time and constant practice to acquire. Get out of doors all you can and always pay attention to the animal life about you. Learn the birds by note as well as by sight.

The man who knows birds by both sight and song has a tremendous advantage over him who does not.

He can single out the specimens he wants by sound, go to them and get them, while his companion simply trusts to luck. Make it your business to look up any "new" notes and find out what they are.

Aside from advantages in collecting, the man who knows the songs and calls of birds, who can recognize their flight, as well as know their plumage and habits, can get 1000 per cent. more enjoyment out of a walk in the woods than the one who notices nothing unless it is called to his attention.

When to Find Birds

By far the best season to see birds and learn them is in the Spring. They are in full plumage and full song, making it easy to find them and also to learn how they look. The scientific collector aims to get at least the male, female and young of the year. Young males are usually similar to the female in coloration and it often takes several years to attain their perfect plumage. No taxidermist, collector or bird student should be without a field glass to distinguish species and to enable him to secure the best; the ones that are in the most perfect plumage.

You will find that birds are much more active a few hours after sunrise than they are during the day. Consequently early morning is the best time to pursue your quest, whatever your motive.

Caution

By caution we mean walking carefully through woods and field, with no unnecessary noise. Let the birds make the noise for you to hear; do not alarm them. We do not, by any means, mean for you to adopt Indian or any other ridiculous tactics, but simply do not "lumber" along, whistling, the way we have seen scores do.

Keep A Record

Every collector, whatever the subject, should keep a record of all his finds. These should be kept in a good substantial notebook, numbering the first specimen you get No. 1, and so on consecutively; whether your specimen be bird, mammal or fish makes no difference, give it its consecutive number. Your specimen may be mounted, kept in a skin or traded, but you have its serial number and can at any time find its data in the proper place in your notebook. After the number, give the place taken and the date, dimensions of the

specimen, etc., after having given the dates of all
the specimens of a day's collecting, you can add any
items of interest connected with the specimens or
others seen, that you care to.   Your book will thus
be very useful and valuable to yourself and may be
useful to others in the future.   It will recall to
your mind, in after years, many interesting facts
that you have forgotten.

Labelling a Specimen

Every scientific skin or mounted specimen should
have its label attached; otherwise it is worthless as
such.   This label should not, as is too often the
case, simply give the birds or animal's name; in
fact, in most cases, that is the least important thing
on a label.   It should have its consecutive number
to correspond to your note book; its place of cap-
ture and date (these two are very important for a
bird's plumage varies a great deal with the season
of the year and also according to the locality in
which it is taken.   You or some one else may want
to study the plumage of a certain bird and, unless
you know the exact place and date the specimen
was taken, it is worthless for study.)   It should
also give the length, expanse and length of wing of
the specimen if it is a bird.   An example of a correct label is given in sketch.

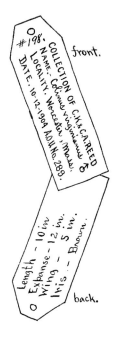

Dovekie

The Sexes of Birds

Every label should, without fail, have the sex of the specimen marked upon it. Scientists of all nations are agreed upon the signs that designate sexes. These are ♂ for male, and ♀ for female, these being the symbols respectively of Mars and Venus. Young birds or animals are designated by yg. following the symbol, or by juv., from the Latin, juvenus, meaning young; this latter is the better form.

The sex of mammals is never in doubt, while that of birds often is and should be accurately determined. The male and female of many species differ greatly in plumage, but in such cases the young birds of either sex very strongly resemble the female and an examination is necessary to determine the sex. The distinguishing masculine organs are the testicles, while those of the female are the ovaries. Both these organs lay in approximately the same positions, namely in the belly near the small of the back. These organs vary greatly in size at different seasons of the year, during the breeding season being large and readily recognized while at other times they may be very small, sometimes requiring a magnifying glass to distinguish them.

To find these organs, cut through the belly walls with your scissors, from the anus diagonally to the base of the lower rib on the right side. With your scapel push the intestines aside and you can see the sexual organs resting on the front of the kidneys. The testicles are a pair of nearly spherical whitish bodies, side by side; the ovaries are a flat, whitish mass of irregular shape, readily recognized when producing eggs, but at other seasons of a fine granular appearance. Both the ovaries and testes are connected with a fine whitish thread to the lower bowel. This will prevent your mistaking the whitish caps of the kidneys, which are present in both sexes, for the testes of the male.

Rocky Mountain Sheep

CHAP. 2--Mounting Birds

We will suppose that you have your specimen before you, and for practice we recommend that you use Blue Jays, English Sparrows or Crows, whichever you can most conveniently obtain.

Tools or Material Necessary

You require very few instruments while learning the art of taxidermy; if, after becoming proficient you wish to continue in the business professionally, you can secure a more expensive outfit. At the start you need:

1. A scalpel or very sharp knife. This is a knife such as surgeons use in operations; you can procure one from any dealer in taxidermist's supplies.

2. A pair of strong, sharp-pointed scissors; surgical ones are the best, although any will answer. For large birds and animals you will also need a pair of bone shears, but you can as well do without these until you become more acquainted with the work.

3. Forceps or Tweezers.—These are very necessary especially in picking over and arranging the
feathers when mounting your bird. Those having sharp points are the best for the work; you can
procure them from your dealer in supplies or at
hardware stores.

4. Cotton; the ordinary cotton batting that you
can purchase at any drygoods store.

5. Sawdust or corn meal; fine hardwood sawdust that you can procure at a cabinet-makers is by
far the best, although fine soft-wood sawdust will
answer. Failing to get either of these, you can
use un-bolted corn meal.

Skinning

First remove the cotton, which you placed in the
bird's mouth when you procured it, and replace it
with a fresh piece. Never attempt to skin a bird
unless you have cotton in its throat for the blood
or juices will be certain to soil the feathers; to be
sure, blood stains can be removed as we shall explain later, but it is far better to avoid them and
you will get better results in your finished work.

Except in tropical countries, a bird will skin the
best, four or more hours after its death. If it is
attempted sooner, the plumage will be very apt to

be soiled for the blood will not have sufficiently
coagulated so as not to run freely. You will find
that a bird killed one day and skinned the next will
make the most satisfactory subject to work upon.

Before commencing to skin your specimen, it is
best to loosen the rigidness of the wings by bending them back so that the shoulders will touch behind the back, bending them carefully so as not to
break the bones; should these bones be broken, it
will not interfere with the successful skinning or
mounting of the specimen, but a good taxidermist
takes pride in not mutilating his specimens.

Place a clean piece of paper upon your work
bench or table and lay your bird upon it with the
head to your left and belly upward. With the
point of the scalpel and your fingers, part the
feathers on the breast and you will find that a
space, nearly devoid of feathers extends from the
breast bone to the anus. Make a clean cut with
your scalpel down the center of this bare space
(from a point slightly below the breast bone to the
vent), taking care to just cut through the skin and
as little as possible into the flesh; practice will
enable you to complete the operation of skinning

The Opening Cut.

without cutting into the flesh at all except to disjoint legs, tail and wings.

Sever leg here.

Grasp the edge of the severed skin on the left side of the breast, with thumb and fore-finger nails (or the tweezers if you prefer) and gradually turn it back, pushing the flesh away from the skin with the blade of the scalpel, which, of course, is always held in the right hand. (We give these instructions for right-handed persons and many of the operations would have to be reversed for a "left-hander.")

The skin on most of our birds separates very easily from the flesh and does not require any cutting; exceptions to this are the ducks and others ot the diving-birds, on which the skin and flesh have to be separated almost entirely by cutting. (It is well to avoid birds of this nature until you are quite proficient with other birds).

It must be borne in mind that from the time you make your first cut, all exposed surfaces either of skin or flesh must be kept sprinkled with the sawdust or meal. This will absorb any moisture or juices and keep the feathers clean.

You will have separated the skin and flesh on your bird for but a short distance before you reach

the junction of the leg with the body. Grasp the
knee-joint with a finger and thumb of the left hand
upon either side, and with the right push the leg up
through the skin so that the entire knee-joint will
be visible and the skin free all about it. Sever the
leg at this joint with the scissors. You now skin
this leg down nearly to the ankle joint, or as far as
the flesh extends; remove all the flesh from the leg-
bone by cutting the tendons near the ankle and
stripping off the flesh. Now go through precisely
the same operation on the opposite side of the bird,
and you will find that it will greatly facilitate your
work if the bird's head is towards you during this
operation.

Having cleaned both leg-bones, thrust them both
back into the skin in their normal position.

Holding the body of the bird by the thighs,
separate, with the fingers, the skin from the flesh
towards its back and tail until your fingers meet on
both sides under the small of his back. You can
now sever the tail, with the scissors, at its junction
with the body taking care not to cut off the ends of
the quills as this would loosen the feathers and let
them fall out.

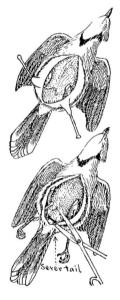

Hawk Owl

Grasp the body by its hips, with the right hand and, with the left, separate the skin from the body, working towards the shoulders until you reach the wing joints. You can easily work your fingers around these joints until they meet; then introduce one point of the scissors and sever the bone near the body.

Continue skinning towards the head, turning the skin inside out the same as you would in taking off a kid glove. When you reach the base of the skull, work the skin over carefully with the thumb nails. pushing first on one side then the other as well as top and bottom. Never pull on the skin in any of the operations but, with the fingers or nails push it apart from the flesh. Immediately upon getting the skin turned over the largest part of the head you will come upon the ears, one on each side and with the skin tucked into a small opening in the skull.

sever
wings

On most all birds up to the size of a crow you can readily pull this skin out of the ear with the thumb and fore-finger; some of the hawks, owls, ducks, etc., require that the skin should be cut as close to the skull as is practicable.

On turning the skin a trifle more over the skull

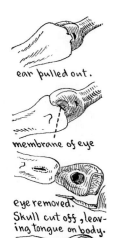

ear pulled out.

membrane of eye

eye removed.
Skull cut off, leaving tongue on body.

3 cuts to remove the brains.

you will come to the eyes; this is one of the most
delicate operations for the beginner. Work the
skin down as far as possible on top of the skull,
between the eyes and on the sides of the head; then
with the left hand draw the skin taut and, with the
scapel, sever the thin membrane in the corner of the
eye. A little practice will enable you to do this
readily without danger of cutting the eye-lid, which
shows faintly through the membrane as a whitish
line. You continue skinning over the skull down
to the very base of the bill.

With the scalpel, or in the case of large birds a
stronger skinning or hunting knife, slice off the
back of the skull, exposing the brains. In doing
this have the bird's skull resting on the bench and
cut through the pony part down to the windpipe;
you can then lift the head and continue cutting
along under the jaws towards the tip of the bill,
this releasing the tongue which will remain attached
to the neck. The body is now entirely free from
the skin and should be laid to one side. Run the
point of the scalpel around the eye, inside the
socket, and you will loosen all the tissues that hold
it in place; you can then easily scoop it out with the

scalpel, taking care not to pierce it as the fluid contained therein will surely soil the bird if you do.
Insert one of your scissor points on the side of the
under jaw, at a point about under the eye, and force
it up until it touches the top of the skull, then
make a clean cut on that side of the skull; do the
same on the other side; then a final cut across the
skull (inside) from eye to eye will release all the
matter contained therein and the brain will come
out whole.

Skinning the wing.

Now, with the right hand, hold the skin firmly
by the wing-bone while, with the fingers of the left
hand, you force the skin back on the wing until the
flesh and muscles of the fore-wing are exposed.
Clean these bones with the scalpel, removing every
particle of meat; also clean off any particles of
flesh that may have been left on any part of the
skin. Turn the legs inside out again and you have
your specimen skinned and all ready to be poisoned.

Arsenic used in the form of a soft soap, as described in Chapter 10 is the best material known
for the preservation of a bird's skin. Of course
arsenic in the hands of careless or very ignorant

persons is dangerous, but it may safely be handled
by any person of ordinary intelligence.

Apply the soap thoroughly to the skin with a
stiff, round brush, taking special pains to well
cover the skull, root of the tail, and leg and wing
bones; next springle the skin, where soaped, with
sawdust or meal so you can handle it and not get
the soap on the feathers.

Fill the cavity of the skull full of cotton and
with the tweezers draw it out into the eye-sockets.

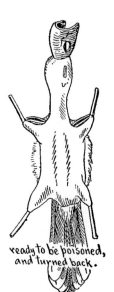

ready to be poisoned,
and turned back.

Pull the legs and wings back into their normal
position from the outside and you have left only
the head to turn back. This is done by working
carefully from the inside with the thumbs and
fingers of both hands; having gotten the skin over
the largest part of the skull you can readily work
it the remainder of the way from the outside.

The feathers of the head will fall naturally and
smoothly into place if the end of a knitting needle,
the square end of a piece of wire or the head of a
pin is inserted through the eye-lid and worked
about on the top and sides of the head.

You now have the skin of your bird in a condition ready to be either mounted or made into a

scientific skin. In our course of personal instruction this usually constitutes the first lesson. If your skin is quite free from tears and cuts you may at once proceed with the mounting or making up a skin; if not, however it will be much better for you to try this lesson over again on another day. When you try your first mounting you should have a skin in as good condition as possible before commencing; therefore it is much better not to make the attempt unless your first effort at skinning is very successful.

Some Exceptional Cases

As you make progress in the art of taxidermy and handle different species of birds, you will soon find that there is a vast difference in the case of operation on various birds. Some have fairly tough skins, like woodpeckers and hawks, while others, as the woodcock and nighthawks, have very tender skins and require very delicate manipulation; a rent once made in such a skin enlarges with alarming rapidity, but a few stitches will mend the worst tears. Some birds, like all pigeons and doves, have feathers very loosely fastened to the skin and they fall out with the least provocation or, in fact, no provocation at all.

passing the skull back through neck

Smoothing head.

Snowy Owl

Continued practice will allow you to handle any
kind of a bird with the loss of comparatively few
or no feathers, and with no cuts or tears in the
skin. A good taxidermist takes pride in doing a
"clean job."

Some birds have very large skulls and small
necks, which will not give enough to allow the
skull to pass through. These require a special
operation, but fortunately such birds are comparatively few in number. All of the woodpeckers skin
"hard" over the head, but they will all go except
the Pileated and Ivory-billed. Many members of
the duck family cannot be skinned over the head in
the usual manner. With such specimens you proceed as previously described until you reach the
base of the skull (and then you will readily see
that you cannot continue further), at which point
you sever the neck. Turn the head back to its normal position, part the feathers along the back or
side of the head and make a lengthwise cut as
shown. The edges of the skin can be pushed apart
and the skull readily passed through this opening,
proceeding the same as though you were working
through the neck. We usually prefer opening a

opening

Skull clean

Sewing up.
LARGE HEADS.
side cut.

head on the side, choosing the side that is the poorer of the two or the side opposite that which is intended to be the front of the completed specimen.

After the head is skinned, brains removed, eyes taken out and skull poisoned and filled with cotton, turn it back and carefully sew the edges of the cut together with close, continuous stitches; be careful not to catch any of the feathers under the thread, and the head will look as well as ever, showing no traces of the cut or thread. If you open your bird on the back of its head, you will find that it will facilitate the work if you have a round hole in your bench in which you can stick the bill of the bird; this holds his head firmly in the position you want it and also allows you two hands to work with.

LARGE HEADS.
Back cut.

Some of the ducks and gannets are among the most difficult of birds to skin. The skin sticks to them as tightly as if glued, and has to be cut away from nearly the whole body; any attempt to push the flesh away from the skin only results in shoving your fingers through the skin, which is inelastic and apparently brittle. Again these birds are always fat and greasy. After skinning you have to "clip" the hide, that is cut off the fat that adheres

to its whole surface. This is a rather tedious process but it has to be done, otherwise in time, the fat
would "stew" through the breast and turn the
feathers a sickly, greasy yellow.

Eagles, swans, loons, geese and large herons
have long wing bones and it is very difficult to
thoroughly clean them from the inside of the skin.
Such wings can best be cleaned by opening them on
the outside; hold back the feathers so as not to cut
any off and make a clean cut through the bare
tract. You can then clean out all the flesh, give
the skin a good coat of arsenic and sew the cut up.
This is always advisable on large birds as it en-
ables you to thoroughly poison just that portion of
the bird that is most frequently attacked by insect
pests.

On large herons and cranes, it is well to make a
cut in the sole of the foot, and by inserting an awl
point under the tendons you can draw them out of
the leg, thus leaving a place for the leg wire and
avoiding danger of splitting the tarsal envelope
when you wire the leg.

Skinning wing of
a large bird.

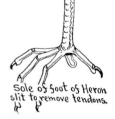

Sole of foot of Heron
slit to remove tendons.

Skinning Game Birds

Grouse, ducks or shore birds can be skinned so as also to save the flesh for eating. A sportsman can thus have his dinner and also have the specimen mounted. Clean the tools to be used, well, and use corn meal in place of sawdust. We usually skin up to the neck with meal then cut the body off and finish skinning with sawdust. The meal will readily wash from the flesh, whereas the sawdust sticks very tightly. We have eaten all kinds of game and believe that the taste of a bird is rather improved than impaired by skinning.

Mounting a Bird

Before you commence to mount a bird, conceive in your own mind the exact position that you wish to reproduce, basing your position from memory of that particular bird as you saw it in life, or upon some good picture of that or a similar bird.

Remember that no live bird is so "ugly" but that he has his graceful lines. All birds whatever their position should have their plumage smooth. Though a bird may be preening itself, with every

feather standing upon end, they will stand on end
smoothly.

Tools and Materials Required

1.   Wire cutters; a pair of parallel pliers with
cutter attached on the side makes the best "all
around" tool of this kind that can be had.   You
can use them for cutters, pinchers and in place of a
leg drill for forcing the wire through the legs of
large birds; a hole through the center of the pliers
allows the wire to pass between the handles so you
can get a perfect grip upon it.

2.   Wire—For practice we should recommend
the getting of half a pound each of Nos. 20, 18
and 16 annealed iron wire.   These will answer for
anything up to jays and kingfishers.   You can get
wire of dealers in taxidermists' supplies or at hardware stores. Following these instructions for mounting birds we give a table of the size wire required
for birds of various kinds, from which you can
decide just what you want for anything.

3.   An eight or ten-inch file with which to point
your wires.

4.   Tweezers, needles, and cotton as before.

5.   A small quantity of excelsior or tow, which
can be procured from your dealer or at a mattress

White-faced Glossy Ibis

shop, and often at a grocery or furniture store.

6.   A ball of cotton twine and a cop; the latter is composed of fine soft cotton thread such as is used in a cotton mill. Your supply dealer can furnish them.

7.   An awl for boring holes in the perches for the leg wires to go through.

Mounting

We will suppose that you have your specimen before you. Skin it, poison the skin, turn it back and smooth the feathers as explained in the instructions for skinning, and remove every vestige of blood or stain from the feathers by means of the water, sawdust and plaster treatment given in the process for making a bird skin.

You will want four wires nine or ten inches in length, and if your specimen is a jay, number 18 will be the correct size. Sharpen one of these wires on both ends and the others on one only.

Take a small wad of excelsior or tow, compress it in the hands to about the size of the original body and wind it firmly with the cotton twine, turning the body and shaping it with the hands as you wind. Don't be afraid of using the string; make the body fairly firm; and above all do not get it larger than the original. Having gotten it as near

the shape of the body you removed as you can, try
it in your bird and draw the skin over it on the
breast; if the edges meet readily, the body is all
right; if not, do not use it,—make another. The
double-pointed wire is to be inserted in the middle
of the larger end of the body and pushed clear
through beyond the small end, turned over into a
hook and drawn back, thus clinching the wire firmly in the body and leaving a section protruding
from the large end for the neck of the bird. In
the case of large birds it is well to use a longer wire
and make a hook long enough so you can draw it
back clear through the body and make a second
clinch.

body
ready to
place in
bird.

Wind a narrow strip of cotton around the neck
wire forming it with the fingers so it will be no
larger or no longer than the neck that you removed;
then wind it smoothly down with the cops.

Now holding your bird up by the beak, insert
the end of the neck wire through the opening in the
belly of your specimen and insinuate it up until the
point of the wire reaches the skull.

The wire should enter the skull from between the
lower jaws; by twisting it between the thumb and
fingers and pushing at the same time, it is forced
through the cotton and finally through the top of
the skull at a point between the eyes and just back
of the upper beak. Push the wire up through the

skull until the cotton wound part reaches the skull.
The body will now perfectly fit in that of the skin
and the neck will be about the proper length.

Wiring the Legs

Insert the pointed end of one of your wires in
the middle of the sole of one foot; by twisting it
between the thumb and fingers you can readily force
it up to the second joint, which corresponds to our
ankle. The wire should pass through the back part
of the leg under the skin. When you have reached
the ankle joint, bend the joint forward so the tarsus and tibia will be in a straight line and hold it
there with the left hand, while with the right you
bore the wire up past the joint. This is easily done
usually the first attempt.

Holding the skin away from the body, push the
leg bone through its opening until you have it
turned completely inside out, the same as when you
first skinned it; now force the wire up until it extends perhaps a half-inch beyond the end of the
leg bone; secure the bones to the wire by winding a
small piece of cotton about both, shaping it so as

wiring leg.

leg bone wound.

also to take the place of the muscles that you removed from the leg.

wiring
of a
small
bird.

The position in which the leg wires are anchored
to the body varies considerably with the position
of the bird, but for a specimen in an ordinary
perching attitude, you should thrust the wire
through the body at a point about midway and a little nearer the breast than the back, hook the protruding end of this wire and clinch the same as you
did the neck wire.   Both legs are of cuurse wired
precisely alike.

Wiring the Tail

During the process of wiring both the legs and
the tail, the specimen lays upon its back upon your
bench.   The fourth wire is pushed through the
roots of the tail from outside, enters the body in
center of the small end and passes out through the
breast where it is turned and clinched; the end protruding beyond the tail is now turned sharply at
right angles to one side and then doubled back upon
itself, from a point slightly outside the outer tail
feathers; it thus forms a platform to hold the bird's
tail in any position desired while drying.

The legs which are now sticking straight out, one on either side of the body, are bent sharply upward where the wires enter the body, until they become parallel.

Draw the edges of the breast cut together and sew it with two stitches (for birds of the size of a jay; larger ones should have more), each stitch being separate and tied of itself.

sewing up.

Bend the legs sharply forward at the heel joint so the feet will be under the breast and the bird balanced in a perching position.

Your specimen is now ready to place upon its stand, and we advise, especially at first, that you mount all your birds on T perches.

Bore two holes in the cross piece about an inch and a quarter apart (for a jay), using your smallest awl. Set your bird on the stand by putting one leg wire through each hole and drawing the bird down until the sole rests on the stand. The bird is now ready to be bent into a life-like position. Of course its wings are not fastened yet and are dangling about, but body, neck and legs are bent in the proper places before the wings are pinned into position. Sketches on this page give a number of positions for the jay with the correct placing of the wires, bending of the neck and legs and tilting the tail for each position. Select the

Sanderling

Black Terns

position you want your bird to occupy before you
commence to mount it and then stick to it.

Pinning Wings Into Position

Having gotten your specimen into the desired
position, you have now to pin the wings in place.
Cut four pieces of your No. 20 wire about two
inches in length and sharpen one end of each (if
you do any number of birds you will find that taxidermists' pins for large birds and insect pins for
birds up to the size of a jay, will be more convenient. Your dealer can furnish both of these.
The large pins come only in one size while you will
want Nos. 3 and 6 of the insect pins).

It makes no difference which wing is put in position first, only you will find that it will facilitate
matters if, when putting up the right wing, the
bird is headed away from you, while in pinning the
left wing he should be head on.

First spread the wing; then fold it seeing that
the feathers properly overlap. Lift the scapulars
or those back feathers that cover the bend of the
wing when it is folded, holding them well up on the
back while you put the wing against the side of the

body, pinning it through the wrist joint (the bend
in the wing). Pull the wing slightly out on the
wire; do not leave it jammed hard down against the
body. Place the tip of the wing on the back or at
the side, as your position may call for, and support
it there by a wire pushed into the flank of the body,
the outer feathers of the wing resting upon this.

With your tweezers carefully pick all the feathers into position. The feathers should lie smoothly
on all parts of the bird, with no open spaces anywhere, especially in front of the bend of the wing.
They should lay smoothly and satisfactorily before
the bird is wound; feathers that are out of place
can be wound down so that they will look all right
but they are apt to "hump" up after the windings
are taken off. The only correct way is to have
them just right before winding at all.

The winding is a delicate operation and is per-
formed with the soft thread on your cops. The
cop shoudl be suspended from the ceiling or some
point above your work by means of a wire pushed
through the small paper cylinder that protrudes
from its large end, and then bent in the form of a
hook with which to suspend it. Be careful to get

the right thread in starting it off the cop, and it
will all run off easily without snarling.

The feathers are already in place as you want
them; the thread is wound on to keep them there,
for as they dry some of them might rise up. The
thread must not be pulled anywhere but simply
laid carefully on. Wind the back first, passing the
thread from one wing wire to the other, back and
forth and across until you have all the feathers
caught down; then wind completely around and
around the bird, each thread catching a different
place on the bird's breast or underparts; a few
turns of the thread around the head and neck (very
carefully made) will complete the task of winding.

If the back of the head or the chin of the bird is
not filled out sufficiently, this can readily be reme-
died by inserting small pieces of cotton through the
mouth or eyelids, as may be most convenient, using
a short piece of wire for this purpose. Steady the
bird by the bill and carefully pull the cotton out of
the head, through the eyes, just sufficiently to make
the lids rounded in a natural position. The eyes
are not put in until the bird is thoroughly dry.

To keep the tail spread evenly as desired, bend a

fine wire as shown in sketch opposite, spread it open in the middle to allow it to slip on the tail; about midway on the tail pinch it together with the fingers and it will keep the feathers just where you want them during the process of drying.

wire to spread tail.

wire in position.

another method.

Art in Mounting a Bird

When mounting a specimen, up to the point of bending it into position, your work is largely or wholly mechanical; but from this point until the bird is completed and ready for exhibition your artistic sense will be called upon. No one will get a perfect bird upon his first attempt unless he be a natural-born taxidermist or artist, and such are very few and far between. But anyone, with continued practice can mount a satisfactory specimen. In this work as well as in any other vocation, "practice makes perfect" so do not be discouraged if your first attempt does not meet your expectations; you have the principle, all you need is the practice.

Drying

The wires and windings are all left on your bird until it is thoroughly dry, which, if placed in a room of ordinary temperature, should take four or five days. When a bird is dry can be judged by the absolute rigidity of the toes and the firmness of

the wings. After telling how to put the eyes in
your specimen, how to properly finish it and how
to make the stands to set it on, we will explain a
number of unusual points and methods necessary
in the mounting of various other kinds of birds.

Putting Eyes in Birds

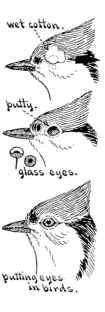

As we have previously said, the eyes are not put
in a bird until it has dried. This is because the act
of doing so is almost certain to disarrange the
plumage. If the eyelids are left round, the eyes
can be put in a position very easily and nicely for
the head skin is dry and will stand handling. With
your forceps, carefully thrust back into the skull
the cotton that is now fiilling the eye hole. Insert
a small piece of wet cotton in each cavity and let
your specimen stand for about a half hour. This
wet cotton is then removed and you will find that
the lids are softened so you can vary their shape
at will. The eyes that you want for a jay are No.
6 brown. It is well to have a small supply of eyes
on hand such as you may want for specimens you
are apt to get. The majority of birds have brown
eyes, but of course that is one of the things that is

made record of when skinning a specimen, and in case of a made-up skin, should be on the tag accompanying the same, so that should anyone desire to mount that skin there would be no doubt as to the color of eye. You can procure eyes at small cost from your dealer in supplies. Chapter 11 shows a chart giving the sizes and styles of eyes commonly used and also an explanation of the sizes and colors used for many birds. An eye should be just a hair larger than is the eye opening of the specimen it is for.

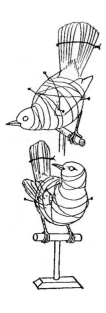

Putty is used for holding the eyes in position. It can be procured at any paint store for a few cents a pound. Black putty is the best for the purpose, but white will answer if you cannot get the other. The putty should be just soft enough so as to be easily squeezed with the fingers; if it is too soft it will be very sticky and requires the addition of a little whiting; if it is too hard it will crumble and needs a drop or two of boiled oil added to it. It is well to procure a few ounces of each of these ingredients at your paint store for you frequently need them as putty hardens rapidly if open to the

air; it should, however, be kept in a closed tin box
and only such quantity taken out as is required.

Having the material ready and your specimen's
eyelids well softened we will proceed with the operation.   Introduce the putty through the eyelids,
with the tweezers, in the form of little pellets, until you have the cavity comfortably filled; then put
the eye in position.   With the point of a needle
draw the lids down so as to cover the rim of the
eye and push back, out of sight, any putty that may
be visible around the edges.   Finally wipe the glass
eye with a moist piece of cotton and it will give it
the lustre of life.

Finishing the Specimens

With your wire cutters cut off the wire that protrudes from the top of the head, the one through
the root of the tail and the two that pass through
the birds wings, sliding the cutters down on the wire
as closely to the skin as possible so that the end of
the wire will be covered with the feathers.   Pull
out, with a twisting motion, the two wires put in
the side of the bird to support the wings, and slide
the bent wire off the tail.   A light dusting with

Swallow-tail Kite.

Screech Owls

a feather duster, always stroking in the direction
of the feathers, will make your specimens ready
to put on its permanent mount.

Right here let me beg you, no matter how poor
or indifferent your first attempt may be, not to
throw it away but keep it for a guide in mounting
the next one. You can see wherein your fault lies
and correct it in subsequent mounts.

Making T Perches

A T perch is composed of but three pieces; a
square base, a round upright set into it and a horizontal crosspiece on the upright. These stands can
be very neatly made and are commonly used for
museum specimens.

For sparrows and birds of like size, make the
base of half inch pine, 2 1-2 in. square, with the
upper edges chambered or cut off, and a 3-8 in.
hole in the middle extending nearly but not quite
through; the upright and cross pieces should each
be 2 in. long, of 3-8 in. doweling or of pine whittled
down to that size. The top end of the upright is
hollowed out to receive the cross piece. Put a touch
of glue on the bottom of the upright, thrust it in
hole in square block; another dab of glue on hollow
of upright and put cross piece on, fastening it with
a brad driven into the upright. These stands can

be made for any size of perching bird, varying only
the dimensions of the stock used.   A stand for a
jay should be 3 in. square at the base and should
have a height of about 3 1-2 in.   If these are only
for temporary stands they are now complete, but if
you wish them for display, give them a coat of
white lead and then varnish.   Natural and artificial
stands and stumps are discussed and explained in
Chapter 12.

Spreading a Birds Wings

It is often desirable, especially in group work, to
have a bird's wings raised or spread; however, we
should never advise spreading a bird of any kind
unless you have a place to suspend it or it is going
into a case to form part of a group.   Spread birds
are more easily damaged and are usually in the
way, unless, as we said, you have a suitable place in
which to suspend them.

Birds to be spread are skinned exactly as before
described, except that of course the wing bones are
all always left in, while a folded bird may often
have the arm bone taken out; indeed, it is often advisable to do this.   The body is made the same and
wound as firmly as possible; the neck wired and
wound with cotton, and inserted in the bird.

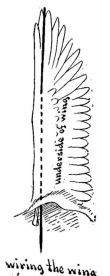

wiring the wing
for spreading.

The next operation is to wire the wings, which has to be done before wiring the legs.

The wing wire should be of the same size or a trifle smaller than the leg wires; its length should be rather more than half the expanse of the bird. For an eagle you would need two No. 10 wires about four feet in length; one end of each of these must be sharpened. With the left hand, grasp the wing at its wrist joint, straightening this joint as much as is possible while you insert the point of the wire under the skin at a point just above the wrist (that is, nearer the tip of the wing) on the under side and force it over the joint, continuing on along the bone and under the skin until it appears inside the skin of the bird. Pass the wire through the body at the large end, at the point where the shoulder bone was anchored on the original body; turn the wire; pass it back again and clinch. It is very important to make a double clinch on each of the wing wires, otherwise the wings are apt to work loose. Wind a little tow or cotton around the wire and arm bone to replace the flesh that was removed and to hold the bone in place. Proceed with the wiring of the legs and tail, and sewing up the cut the same as

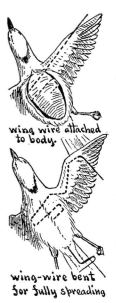

wing wire attached to body.

wing-wire bent for fully spreading

outlined before. Place your bird on a stand, bearing in mind that if it is to be suspended as if flying the legs will be bent up under the breast, while if it is to be placed on a stump the legs will be in a normal perching position.

Bend the wings upward and backward at the shoulder close to the body, forward at the elbow joint and backward again at the wrist, the amount of bend depending upon whether you want the bird with the wings full spread, half spread or just raised.

Insert two pins or sharpened wires on each side of the body under the wings. These are to wind to. Bend the head and tail as you want them, pick the feathers into position with the tweezers and make sure that all the wing feathers lap the right way.

Wind the under part of the body, passing the thread from side to side about the pins inserted for that purpose; it is also well to insert a wire between the shoulders on the back, and wind from this around the breast; this holds the scapulars in position. Fill out the head if it needs it, form the eyelids into shape and wire the tail. The wing feathers are to be kept in correct position by means of two

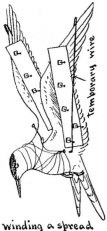

Winding a spread bird.
Paper pinned on each side of each wing.

strips of heavy paper or thin card, fastened to each
wing, one above and one on the under side. They
are held in place by shoving pins through the wing
and both papers; a thin slice of a cork stopper inserted on the point of each pin and pushed down
against the feathers will hold it very firmly.

Herons and Other Long-Necked Birds

The neck that you manufacture on your excelsior
body should be nearly or quite as long as the one
you removed, whatever the position a bird is to be
placed in. When a heron sits, as it usually does,
with its head drawn down on its shoulders, its neck
is not shortened in the least, but is bent downward
and then upwards and back upon itself as illustrated in the heron positions on sketches on this page.
It is quite a clever job to smoothly wind the long
neck of a heron. Carefully and as evenly as possible, wind cotton along the wire, shaping it and
tapering it to the size and length of the original.
Then take perhaps up to a dozen turns with your
cotton twine around the body and neck, passing
the string around the small end of the body diagonally up and around the top end of the neck,
back and forth several times; this firmly attaches
the neck winding to the body. preventing it from

Osprey

slipping up on the wire. Finish winding the neck smoothly with your cops. It will be difficult at first but with practice you can hold the body suspended by the end of the neck wire, held between the thumb and fingers of the left hand. Twist on the wire, thus revolving the body and neck, and with the right hand spin the cops up and down and around the neck until you have it perfectly smooth.

Wiring the Legs of Walking Birds

wiring legs of a walking bird.

If your bird is to be in a walking position, the foot that is back should be resting on the toes with the sole above the ground. It would not look well to have the leg wire showing from the center of the sole to the base and in order to avoid this, run the wire in this leg through the middle toe from the second joint up through the sole and as usual up into the body.

Birds Standing on One Leg

If your bird is standing in this position, when finished you will cut off the wire in the raised leg where it protrudes through the sole. Therefore the wire in the other leg should be heavier and double clinched in the body as it has to support double weight.

Birds With Peculiar Attitudes

PUFFIN

LOON.

Nearly all species of birds have attitudes that are characteristic. I would advise anyone to study live birds all he can, especially as regards the different positions they will take; if you are an adept at sketching, draw off different positions of various birds as you see them. Study well the positions of the birds in this book. We are perfectly familiar with every bird shown and can vouch for the accuracy of either drawings or mounted specimens. I will call attention to a few points that you want to know at the start. You will notice that a duck's body and, in fact, those of all diving birds are flattened rather than compressed; their legs are set wider apart. Grebes, Loons and Auks cannot stand upon the sole of the foot but rest upon the whole tarsus or heel, apparently as though sitting upon their tail. Their legs are anchored to the body a trifle nearer the smaller end than are the legs of most birds; the legs must then be bent backward and then sharply forward at the ankle joint, leaving this joint in close proximity to the tail. A similarly shaped bird, the Puffin, does stand erect on its feet, although it is often pictured as sitting upon the heel and more often mounted that way.

Mounting Collossal Birds

Birds of the size and character of the Ostrich require special methods both of skinning and mounting. In skinning the cut is made from the breast bone to the vent, and then another one is made across the abdomen and extending down the inside of each leg to the sole of the foot. The skinning of the body and neck is identical with that of a small bird except that it is almost necessary to suspend the body from strong hooks as soon as the legs are disjointed, allowing the skin to hang down, and greatly facilitating its removal. All the tendons and muscles are taken out from the back of the legs through the cut you have made. It would be almost physically impossible to run a rod through the leg of an ortrich as we do in other birds; then again we could not anchor it to the body rigid enough to hold his weight.

Frame for Ostrich.

We have to build what is termed a "manikin" for such large birds. This is a completed form with leg rods all in and bolted to the base, ready to throw the skin over.

We first get out a center board about the size and

shape of the longitudinal cross section of his natural body. This must be strongly cleated and on
each side have a piece of 2 x 4 joist about a foot
long firmly screwed. These are put on in the proper place to receive the leg rods, and a hole just the
size of the leg rod bored down through the center
of each. For leg rods you will want half inch material cut to just the length of his leg plus the
thickness of the base he is to stand upon. You will
want about three inches of each end of these rods
threaded to receive nuts. The neck rod should be
about 3-8 in. in diameter; both this and the leg rods
be bent at the proper places before fastening to the
body. The leg wires are fastened to the body by a
nut and washer both above and below the joist;
they are fastened to the base in the same manner.
The neck rod may be fastened to the frame by a
number of heavy staples driven through the board
and clinched. Sketch on preceding page shows
clearly the form of the rods and method of attach-
ment. The body is now shaped with excelsior,
wound very tightly to each side of the frame, and
the neck is smoothly wound with tow. It is well to
give both the body and neck a final coating of clay

Manikin complete

to smoothen them and accentuate the curves and hollows.

Place the skin on your manikin, carefully insinuating the neck into that of the bird. The neck rod should be of just sufficient length to rest inside the skull. Pack the inside of the skull about the rod with clay, and also model some about the skull and upper portion of the artificial neck; then carefuly sew up the cut through which the head was skinned. The leg rods should fit in the back of the legs of your specimen, taking the place of the tendons that you removed. Wire the upper leg bones to the rod, wind with tow and give a covering of clay to represent the muscles.

You must now sew up the breast cut, the legs and cut across the abdomen, using a large sailmaker's needle and waxed twine. The eyes can be immediately put in, modelling the shape with clay and then inserting the eyes.

The wings are pinned in the same manner and the feathers wound the same as on smaller birds.

Crow (Partly albino)

Black-backed Gull

Relaxing Dried Skins for Mounting

When a collector is away from home, he usually makes all his specimens into skins, even though they are to be mounted afterward. Such skins have to be relaxed so that they will be as soft as when first taken from the birds before they can be mounted.

The older a bird skin gets, the drier it becomes and the longer it takes to relax it. Many methods have been and are used for the relaxing of bird skins; we have had long experience with all of them but for the past 12 years have used but the one described hereafter, considering all others but half-way measures. Winding wet cloths about the specimen, or putting it in damp sawdust, answers fairly well but does not get at all points of the skin and is more apt to start the feathers than the following:

Remove as much of the cotton filling as possible through the breast, working it out very carefully with the tweezers and fingers so as not to tear the skin, which is now very brittle. You can usually get all the cotton out, but if not it does not matter.

Immerse the whole specimen in a pail of lukewarm
water, moving it about a few seconds to remove air
bubbles and insure all parts of the skin being wetted. Float a piece of board on the water to keep
your specimen fully immersed. A specimen up to
the size of a crow will usually become relaxed in
12 to 16 hours, so if it is put into water at night it
should be ready to mount the next day. Birds the
size of a crow or over should have the legs and feet
wrapped in wet cloths for about twelve hours before
placing the specimen in water. The skin of the
feet and legs is so dry and tough that otherwise
they would not be relaxed enough to bend freely
when the remainder of the skin was ready for
mounting.

Rub the skin inside thoroughly with the thumb
nails, or if it is a large bird scrape it with a knife to
remove fibre or fat. Rub the inside of the neck and
head with a knitting needle, inserted through the
neck or eye as is most convenient. Then put your
skin back into a pail of fresh warm water, and leave
for a couple of hours longer.

Now turn the skin inside out, working very carefully for the skin will not yet give as much as that

of a fresh bird. Thoroughly rub the neck and head
with the thumb nails, paying particular attention to
the parts that seem the hardest; dip the skin in the
water at frequent intervals so as to work it into
the skin as you rub.

Turn the skin back to its normal position and
squeeze between the hands so as to get it as dry as
possible; do not wring it; just a simple squeeze.
Place the skin in a jar or deep dish containing just
enough naptha to cover it; move it about for a few
seconds to be sure that the skin will be thoroughly
saturated. Leave it in the naptha for about thirty
minutes; the object of this bath is to remove any
grease that may still be upon the skin and to render
it more easy to dry off.

CORMORANT.

PETREL

Remove it from the naptha and again squeeze the
skin as dry as you can. Unless you are working on
a white bird, or one with an immaculate breast, we
would advise you to dry it as thoroughly as possible in sawdust, dusting and brushing it into the
feathers to absorb the moisture; then use plaster in
the same manner to bring the feathers out as fluffy
as they were on the live bird.

White birds should not be put in the sawdust but

directly into the plaster; bear in mind that plaster
hardens very rapidly upon getting wet or moist, so
you must work quickly, keeping your bird moving
and continually shaking and brushing the plaster
out of the feathers; if it is allowed to stand on the
feathers in any one place more than a second or two
it is apt to stick and be very difficult to remove.
Plaster is one of the best friends of the taxidermist
but it has to be handled with skill and speed.

Kingfisher.

If you have thoroughly worked and scraped the
skin and dried it well, it will now be in as good a
condition as when first taken off the bird.

Fill the skull with cotton, soap the skin well and
it is already to mount the same as a fresh bird.
Very greasy birds such as ducks or gannets we
usually soften up in warm soapy water. A skin
that is so dirty as to be apparently worthless can
usually be brought out in good condition.

Woodcock.

MAKING A BIRD SKIN

The object in making a bird skin is to keep the specimen for all time. It has scientific value for study purposes and can, if desired, be mounted at any time. For a systematic and diagnostic study of the plumage, skins are always used when procurable because they are easily handled without injury, while a mounted specimen becomes utterly ruined after much handling.

Tools Necessary

1.—Brush for cleaning feathers. This is a stiff bristle brush resembling a large tooth brush. You can procure one of a dealer or from most druggists.

2.—Needles and thread. Any medium sized needle will do but a surgical one is best. You can get these from dealers in supplies or druggists. For thread we recommend a spool of white silk and one of white linen.

3.—A plentiful supply of cotton and a box of plaster-of-paris will complete the necessities for making a bird into a skin.

Mockingbird
(With painted background and natural surroundings)

Cleaning the Feathers

After you have skinned a bird, whether you are to mount it or put it into a skin, you must first be sure that the feathers are entirely free from stains of any character.

Blood stains are most easily removed by applying luke-warm water with a piece of cotton; keep rinsing the cotton off, or take fresh pieces until you can wipe over the feathers without getting any stain on the cotton. Do not wet the feathers any more than necessary except on the spot you wish to remove, as they must be dried out again. This drying of the feathers can be accomplished most readily by the continued application of sawdust, working it into the feathers with your brush until the bulk of the moisture is removed; then dust the spot with plaster, applied with the brush until it is thoroughly dry. The plaster and sawdust must all be shaken or brushed out of the plumage before the next operation.

If your bird seems to be dirty or the feathers gummed-up, as is often the case with hawks or owls, you will find that they will clean best with soap and water, afterwards drying them the same as before.

Flicker

Redhead Woodpecker

Making the Skin

See to it that the feathers of your bird all lie smoothly in their proper places, picking them into position with the tweezers. Stretch each wing and allow it to fold back again, making sure that all the feathers properly overlap. Inserting your tweezer points between the eyelids slightly pull the cotton. with which you have filled the skull, out so that it will hold the eyelids in a natural and round position.

In making up birds up to the size of a Blue Jay, the wing bones may or may not be tied together as you wish, but on birds larger than this, it is poor practice not to do so. For our part, we always tie the wing bones together even in making a hummingbird skin; it makes the skin stronger and also insures that the feathers between the shoulders will lie naturally and smoothly. Tie the two wing bones together, inside the skin, so that the shoulder joints will be a little closer together than they were in the specimen before it was skinned.

For a cabinet specimen, one that will in all probability always remain as a skin, it is best practice to make them with a splinter of wood or a wire

Wing-bones tied to make a skin.

extending from the base of the skull to the root of
the tail. Cut a splinter of wood or the twig of a
tree (a quarter of an inch or less in diameter) of a
suitable length to reach from the skull to the base
of the tail when your specimen is laid in a normal
position. Commencing at the head end of your
stick, wind it with cotton, thinly on the neck (which
must be no larger than the original) and more heav-
ily on the rear end, always keeping the cotton fluffy
and springy. The body *must not* be larger than the
one you removed from the specimen.

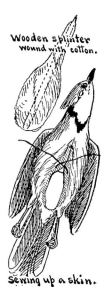

Wooden splinter
wound with cotton.

Sewing up a skin.

This cotton-wound splinter is now inserted into
the neck and body of your bird and the edges of the
skin drawn together over the breast and fastened
together with a single stitch, for birds no larger
than a Blue Jay. Larger birds may require more
stitches. Lay the bird in the hollow of your left
hand, belly down, and with your right raise the two
wings, pressing them together over the back so as
to be sure no cotton is between the shoulders or el-
bows. Now pass your specimen from hand to hand,
keeping the wings well on the back and gradually caressing the feathers into position. Your object is to make your skin look like a dead bird with

feathers smooth and the bill extending horizontally
in front, forming a straight line with the back and
tail. Never allow a bird's bill to tilt up at an angle
in a completed skin.

Lay your specimen carefully down upon its back,
then cross its legs and tie them together at the
point where they cross. Leave the ends of this
thread long enough so that you can attach a label
to it.

Skin
in
paper
Cylinder.

Roll up a paper *cylinder* a trifle longer than your
specimen and of a diameter equal to that of his
greatest girth. (You can hold this cylinder in form
by tying a thread about its middle).

Caress your bird from hand to hand again, making sure that all feathers, especially those on the
shoulders lay smoothly, then carefully slide it into
the cylinder head first. Never use a paper *cone* in

Skin in tin form.

making skins; it makes them hollow-chested and
pot-bellied, with no semblance to grace. Good skins
can also be made by wrapping them in thin layers
of cotton batting, but I think the use of cylinders
the most practical and certainly the specimens are
less liable to injury.

Unusual Forms for Skins

These instructions as given apply to nearly all the land, or perching birds, grouse, hawks, and owls. Some birds, especially those with long necks or legs require special treatment as to the best form in which to leave the finished skin. Obviously it would not do to make a Blue Heron skin with its long neck stretching a couple of feet in front of the body and the legs as much behind. This is overcome by doubling the legs up against the breast and folding the neck down over the back (after it has been carefully and smoothly filled with cotton). Some collectors fold the head and neck back under the wing; this is all right, for compactness, when the skin is to be mounted, but for cabinet specimens they are far better with the head over the back, and fastened by means of a string through the nostrils passing through the body and tied to the legs.

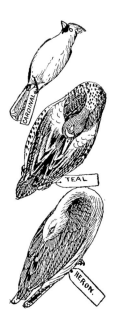

Most ducks make a neater skin, and one less liable to injury if the neck is folded over the back; the same can be said of the larger sandpipers.

Birds having a large and conspicuous crest, such as cardinals, jays, pileated woodpeckers, trogons, etc., should be made into skins with the head turned on one side but with the bill pointing as nearly straight forward as possible.

Hanging "Dead Game" Birds

Winding a hanging bird.

You may have occasion to hang a bird as though it were dead. Many sportsmen like to have their trophies so mounted. The specimen is to be skinned and wired in the usual manner, except that the wings must be wired as for spread birds.

A bird may be hung breast out, back out or on its side. In case you are mounting but one bird, we think they usually look the best the latter way, but it depends largely upon the markings of the bird. Always mount your specimen to show it off to the best advantage. If you hang a pair of birds together it is well to mount one on the side and the other breast out.

The wings being properly wired, will easily bend to the desired position and stay there.

The birds must be fastened to a temporary board by driving a stout wire through the middle of their bodies into the board. Drive pins around the birds very obliquely, smooth their feathers well and wind by passing the cops from one pin to the other.

Positions for hanging birds are well illustrated by the marginal sketches on this page.

CHAP. 3--Mounting Animals
Part 1--Small Mammals

The mounting of mammals can best be divided
into two parts: small, such as squirrels and rodents,
and carnivorous animals up to the size of a fox or
coyote. These are mounted by the semi-modeling
process as will be described in the following pages;
large mammals above the size of a fox, and short-
haired animals like many of the dogs are mounted
by the full modeling process as described in the
next Part.

The first cut.

Skinning

We will take for our subject for this lesson, a
gray squirrel.

You will have at hand, ready for use, a scalpel;
scissors; large scissors or bone shears; a box of fine
sawdust, lacking which you can use corn meal.

As in the cast with birds it is better not to attempt skinning for a few hours after the death of
the subject, or until it has relaxed from the "rigor
mortis" that sets in soon after death. Bend the
legs of your specimen wide apart so as to relax all
the joints. Make your opening cut from between
the forelegs, down through the middle of the breast

Gray Squirrel
(A section of a log makes an excellent base for an animal)

to the vent. Skin each side of this cut until you disclose the hind legs. A small animal skins easily, usually with the fingers and with very little cutting. Push the leg up inside the skin and work your fingers so as to skin entirely around it; you can then sever it near the hip joint. Grasp each hind leg in turn, and by pulling on it and pushing away the skin you can readily turn the legs inside out down to the ankle joint. Remove all the flesh from these bones, with the scissors and scalpel, but do not disjoint the bones at the knee.

Skin around the back of your subject, from both sides until your fingers will meet. Cut across the vent with your scalpel and you will come to the junction of the tail with the body.

The bony skeleton of the tail is now to be pulled out of its covering, entire. Grasp the body with your right hand about the roots of the tail, and place the points of your scissors, one on either side of the bony skeleton that is visible and then brace the points against the back edge of your bench. Do not cut with the scissors, or even pinch, but just simply let them close against the tail bone so that the skin cannot slip through when you pull with the

right hand; you will find that the tail will slip out
easily without injury to the skin. The tails of
many animals up to the size of a fox can be skinned
in this way. With some animals, like cats or rats
the tail cannot be pulled out but must be split the
entire length on the under side and then skinned.
Of course, in this case, you have to sew the cut up
again, so it is best not to split the tail on any animal that you think can be removed without.

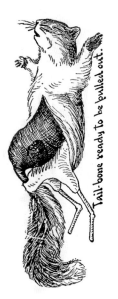

Tail-bone ready to be pulled out.

You now have the entire lower portion of the
body separated from the skin and have reached the
fore legs. Skin around these and cut them off near
the body; clean, the same as you did the hind legs.
Continue skinning up the neck until you reach the
ears. Sever these close to the skull and then skin to
the eyes. By stretching the skin slightly, you can,
through the thin membrane that connects the eye-
lid and skull, see the outline of the lid, which appears as a straight whitish line. Cut between this
and the skull and you will avoid danger of cutting
the eyelid. Continue your skinning down over the
head until you have entirely severed the skin from
the body at the nose.

You now have the skin entirely separated from

the body and turned inside out. Clean off any
pieces of flesh or fat that may be on the skin, and,
with the scissors very carefully cut about the lips,
removing the gristly substance that is to be found
there on all animals; try not to cut through the skin
and be careful not to cut off and loosen the ends of
the "whiskers" on each side of the upper lip. Now
thoroughly poison the skin with your arsenical soap,
sprinkle it with sawdust and turn it right-side out
again. It is best to roll the skin up and place it in
a closed box or else do it up in paper while you are
cleaning the skull and making the body for it. This
will prevent the skin from drying; it can also be
left over night and be in good condition to work on
the next day if you wish. It will probably take
you an hour or so to get the body ready to put the
skin on.

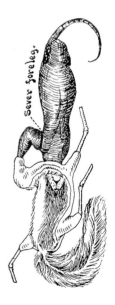

Cleaning the Skull

Cut off the end of the skull just back of the ears,
using the skinning knife for small animals and the
meat saw for large ones. This will leave the brains
exposed and they can readily be scooped out with
the point of the knife. Remove the eyes with your
scalpel and clean every vestige of meat from the
skull. It will be best if you can now put the skull

in an oven and dry it for fifteen minutes, although
this is not necessary.

Sharpen a No. 14 wire on both ends (for gray
squirrel) and thrust one end in the brain cavity,
through the skull so as to come out one of the nostril openings; bend the end sharply back, hook
shaped, and draw it back so the point will enter
through the other nostril. The wire should be doubled long enough so as to enter the brain cavity
again, while the bend will fill up the end of the
nose. Mix a small quantity of plaster and squeeze
some into the skull cavity; this will hold the wire
firmly. Put some plaster also on the nose and cheek
to replace flesh or cartilage removed. Set the eyes
in plaster and build over them a trifle.

Skull cleaned.

wire attached to
skull.

body
ready to
insert.

Making the Body

Wind up a body of excelsior slightly smaller than
the one removed and of the same length, winding it
fairly hard and smooth and try to keep as closely
as possible to the form of the original. This will
be wound with cotton string around the body end-
wise as well as crosswise. Thrust the wire, which
is attached to the skull, completely through this
body, from end to end and clinch, making the
body, from the tip of the nose to the end, just the

same length that your specimen was from his nose
to the root of the tail. Wind a little tow around the
junction of the skull with the neck, and also a thin
layer on the back, winding both down smoothly with
the cops. Whatever the position of your animal is
going to be, bend the body into approximately the
shape that it is to occupy. If you want your squirrel sitting up with a nut in his paws, bend the neck
upward, the head horizontal and put a sharp graceful curve on the remainder of the body.

Insert the body into your specimen (and if you
have left it rolled up over night it will be best to
give it another coat of soap first) insinuating the
head up through the neck to its proper position.
The body should now just fill the skin and when
smoothed down the back, the tail should come in its
proper position at the end.

Number 14 wire is the proper size for the four
legs and the tail. You will want four pieces a foot
long, sharp on one end, and one piece about 18 in.
long, sharp on one end and rounded on the other,
this last one being for the tail. Wire the fore legs
first, running the wire through the sole of the foot,
up through the back of the leg under the skin until

wiring the legs of
a squirrel.

Flying Squirrels
(The upper squirrel suspended by a wire fom the stump)

it appears inside. Turn the leg inside out down to the wrist joint and wind about the bone and wire with tow, winding it firmly with cops to conform with his natural leg; this should be wound way to the end of the bone so as to complete the leg to its junction with the body. Insert the point of the wire at the spot corresponding to the shoulder and push it through the body, pulling the leg down on the wire sufficiently to allow the latter to extend through about three inches on the opposite side. Turn the wire long enough to draw back through the body and clinch again. Wire the hind legs in precisely the same way, winding them to their proper shape and clinching the wire through the body twice. Dip the rounded end of the tail wire into your arsenical soap can; insert this and into the opening of the tail and you will find it will readily push the whole length; if it sticks at any point, a little judicious twisting of the wire, while holding the skin of the tail firmly at the obstruction, will easily force it through.

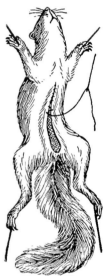

Sewing up the cut.

When the rounded end brings up against the tip of the tail, twist it as though you were using an awl, and you can bore right through. Push the

wire through sufficiently far to enable you to stick
the pointed end in its proper place in the end of
the body; push the wire back through the body
so the end will appear on the breast; make a long
turn and draw it back, clinching a second time
where the point appears again (this should be about
on the rump).

Your specimen is now all wired, but the legs are
sticking straight from the body. Bend them to correspond to the position you have selected for your
animal, and we should advise for your first attempts
that you take some of the illustrations that we show,
for models, for you can readily see just how to do
your work to accomplish a certain result. If your
squirrel is to be sitting up, see to it that he sits upon his heels. Nothing looks so disgusting or un-
natural as to have a squirrel sitting practically upon its tail with his legs sprawled out in front, yet
this is the way that, even now, the majority of professional taxidermists do their work. We want you
to aim to do perfect work; to imitate nature. Do
not let the dollar behind your work look so large
that you can see nothing else; this is a common
mistake with taxidermists.

A wisp of tow around the junction of each leg
with the body will fill up the slight hollow that is
usually left there. You can now sew the opening
cut together, sewing continuously from one end to
the other, always entering the needle from the skin
side. Instead of putting a knot in the end of the
thread it is better to tie the first stitch, while the
last one is fastened by taking several half-stitches
about the last stitch.

Your specimen is now ready to place upon its permanent stand. No neater or more appropriate
stand can be made for squirrels than natural stumps
fastened on a sanded stand for the table or on a
shield to hang on the wall. See that the eyelids of
your specimen are in their proper place and, if
necessary, pin them there. For the first three or
four days, while your squirrel is drying, it will be
well to pinch the ears into shape so they will dry
without any shriveling.

Larger animals always have the ears skinned and
tin inserted, but those of squirrels and other small
rodents dry best with nothing in them.

Be sure that the hair all lies smoothly. The body of your animal is hard enough to withstand any shrinkage of the skin, yet it can be pinched with the fingers to accentuate any curves desired; by clever manipulation, very natural specimens can be made. If you are to have a nut in the specimen's paws, put it in before drying, cutting the wires off just short enough to insert in holes bored in each side of the nut. Many taxidermists sew up the mouths of small animals from the inside as soon as they are skinned. This answers very well for commercial taxidermy, but the results cannot compare to those obtained by pinning the lips to the plaster form. Squirrels, especially, always show their front teeth and should, also, when they are mounted. Several times a day, for three or four days, while the squirrel is drying you should run the hand down the tail, the wrong way of the fur; this will keep it standing on end and give the tail the fluffy appearance of life. On page 94 is a well mounted squirrel, in a correct position, as he sits on a log eating a nut.

Large Mammals

The following instructions apply for animals
from the size of a fox, up; and for very short-
haired smaller animals. A fox or long-haired dog
can be mounted by either method, commercial taxidermists usually using the preceding, while museum
taxidermists, having more time at their command,
use the follwoing which unquestionably is the best.

Skinning

The opening cut is made from between the fore
legs to the anus; another cut across the breast down
the inside of each fore leg to the ankle joint; a
third cut is made across the abdomen and down the
inside of each hind leg. The skinning is then proceeded with as before, but the legs are skinned way
down to the last joint and the bones dislocated and
taken out. If the tail can be pulled out as described
in the foregoing instructions, do so, but most animals that are mounted in this way require that the
tail be split the whole length on the underside before it can be skinned.

The ears should also be skinned, out, that is, the
skin on the back of the ear should be separated

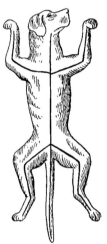

Opening cuts to
skin a large
animal.

Weasel (Winter Fur)
Raccoon (Cork-bark Stump)

from the cartilage. This is done from the inside of
the skin, turning the ear inside out, and pushing the
skin away from the cartilage with the nails or handle of the scalpel. They usually skin quite easily
and seldom require cutting with a knife.

The skin is now cured with arsenical soap if you
are going to mount it immediately, or put into the
salt bath as described in Chapter 10 if you are to
keep it a number of days before mounting. The
whole skin of any animal may be salted as described for deer scalps on page 127, and will then
keep indefinitely and be ready for mounting at any
time upon soaking the skin in water. Of course, you
will see the necessity of taking a number of measurements; the more the better. You want (a) the
entire length of the animal; (b) from nose to back
of skull; (c) from back of skull to shoulder joint;
(d) from shoulder to hip joints; (e) from shoulder
to root of tail; (f) width of body at shoulders; (g)
width at hips; (h) girth back of fore legs; (i)
girth in front of hind legs; (j) girth of neck back
of ears; (k) at base; (l) height of animal at fore
shoulder; (m) height at hind shoulder or hip.

With these measurements you cannot go far

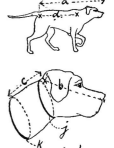

Measurements
of an animal.

astray as to the size of the body, but you still need a drawing, even a crude one, showing the location of prominent muscles, ribs or hollows.

Disjoint the two forward legs at the shoulder joint and the hind ones at the hip joint. The flesh and muscles are all to be cleaned from these, using the scissors or scalpel as may be the most convenient. They must then be thoroughly poisoned with the soap, and set aside until we have the frame ready to put them on.

Wooden centerboard for body.

Method of attaching leg rods to block.

Another method (with staples).

Making the Framework for a Manikin

We will now confine our instructions to the mounting of a pointer dog, the different steps of which are clearly shown in sketches. All other animals are modeled in the same manner, the only difference being in the size and shape of the body and size of rods or wires. Very large animals such as from a horse to an elephant have a hollow framework of wood in place of using so much excelsior. Otherwise they are modeled the same.

You will want six three-sixteenth inch rods and their length will depend on whether you prefer to have them threaded for nuts or attach them to the frame with staples. A wire of this size can be at-

tached in either way, while any of the larger rods,
1-4 inch up should be threaded. The sketch on this
page shows the method of attaching the wire either
way. We usually use staples on animals of this
size so will make the following directions to conform. You will want your rods each about 36
inches in length.

Make a centerboard of inch stock, the size and
shape to correspond to the outline of your specimen's body. Nail blocks of wood about two inches
thick on each side of the centerboard at points
to correspond to the joints of the shoulder and
hips.

Fasten the wire to the dog's skull, as with a squirrel, and fix it firmly with a dab of plaster inside
the skull, covering the wire. Fasten it to the centerboard by driving staples around the bent wire,
being sure that the distance from the shoulder joint
to the base of the skull corresponds to your measurements. Wire each leg bone to its rod and bend
to the shape to correspond to that of your finished
specimen, the wire passing up along the back of
the bones. Bend a loop in the end that projects beyond the upper end of the bone and fasten with

Framework for a
Pointer dog.

Framework wound
to shape.

Covered with clay.

staples to the leg blocks. Fasten your specimen
upright on a temporary base. (See sketch). If it
were put on a finished base at this time, the latter
would get scratched or soiled during succeeding
operations.   Be sure that the centerboard comes
very nearly to your measured heights of your specimen, from the base. Staple the tail wire to the
centerboard and cut it off to its required length. If
your work is correctly done you can, in your imag-
ination, see the form of your specimen from this
framework of bone, wire and wood.

Exceptional Cases

If you are mounting an animal that requires a
neck rod of a quarter-inch or more, it will be best
to fasten the skull to the centerboard by means of
a neck piece of wood, similar to that used for
mounting a deer head. (See Chap. 4). This neck
piece may be made in one or several pieces to conform to the position of the head. It makes a more
substantial framework and one easier to make for
large specimens. The legs in elephants are made
of straight pieces of joist, dispensing with both
bones and rods.

Elk.

Forming the Body

The body, neck and legs must now be formed of excelsior, winding it tightly to the frame, to conform to the animal's true shape, but of slightly smaller dimensions to allow for the coat of plaster that is to be applied, and for the skin. The tail and legs will be smoother if tow is wound on instead of excelsior.

The covered framework should now look very respectable, and begin to give a good idea of what the finished product is to be. The muscles are not reproduced until the next stage, but the general form should be correct.

Covering the Manikin

This can be done with plaster, clay or papiermache. Most taxidermists use clay, chiefly because it is more easily and quickly worked, especially by the unskilled workman. We prefer either papiermache or plaster and think the results are more permanent and satisfactory. Cover the entire manikin from head to tail with plaster, building up the muscles and points as indicated by the drawings and measurements of the original. Remember that plaster hardens quickly, so work fast and don't mix larger doses than you can handle. By mixing up a small pail or dipper full many times you will get

Antelope.

Red Fox (On artificial rock)
Ocelot (On natural stump)

much better results than if you mix a large quantity and try to cover the whole form at once.

Put the plaster on as smoothly as possible and
scrape away for the hollows and build up for the
muscles, remembering that everything wants to be
a little more prominent in the manikin than you
wish it to be in the finished specimen.

Set the eyes in plaster, taking care that they are
looking slightly forward, as all animals do in life.
Fashion the nose, dig out the nostrils, and make the
lips; we can assure you that these operations will
give you a chance to exercise your ingenuity and
display your artistic ability. Your work, now, with
a little scraping and smoothing, should look like
a Pointer dog, lacking only the ears and hair.

A finely modeled manikin can be made equal to
any sculptor's work; the animal is all there save
for its ears and feet, and the outlines of the hair.
It is not necessary, however, to make it as smooth
as if it was not going to be covered. Frequently
time, plaster and weight can be saved by not covering all of the excelsior; especially is this true
when mounting long-haired large animals. The
mounting of a short-haired dog is one of the most

Mountain Sheep

8

difficult works of taxidermy and we would strongly
advise against your undertaking it until you have
had your practice on smaller animals by the pre-
vious method, and also on shaggy ones by this
method.   Do not "tackle" the most difficult job
first, for unless you are a wonder, failure will be
very disheartening; the more so on account of the
time consumed.   We have outlined the steps as fully
as possible, but taxidermy is an art and art can be
developed by nothing except practice.

Putting on the Skin

Your manikin is now completed with all the muscles showing, and finished down to the last joint on
all the legs, which of course, must be sufficiently
elevated from the base to allow the feet to be placed
under them.

The skin should be thoroughly relaxed; if you
have not allowed it to dry up, a good coating of arsenical soap will put it into good condition.   If
dried, soak the skin in water as described for deer
scalps under "mounting heads."   Short-haired dogs
or members of the deer family do not require that
the hair should be dried out before putting the skin
on the manikin, but if your specimen has long hair,
like a shepherd or Newfoundland dog, bear, etc., it
will be necessary to thoroughly dry the hair or fur;

Mountain Lion.

be sure and get all the sawdust out of the hair before you put it on the manikin, otherwise you will find sawdust sifting out of your specimen for years after.

You must now cut a thin piece of sheet lead to conform to the shape of each ear, cutting it, of course, a trifle smaller as it is to go inside. Place these in position before putting the skin on the subject. We use sheet lead for animals having large, short-haired, flexible ears rather than tin such as we use on deer and moose. While not as stiff as tin, it can be bent to the proper shape much more readily.

Place the skin in position on the form. The backs of all the feet should be cut with the scissors so as to allow them to fit about the wire. Fill the ankle joints with clay (mixed as per instructions in Chap. 10) so they will make good connections with the lower ends of the legs on the manikin. You now have a good, long, tedious task before you,—that of sewing up the cuts on the legs and belly. For the pointer dog, black linen thread used double and thoroughly waxed, will be best. Larger animals often need strong hemp twine for this purpose. Start at the bottom of one of the legs, using a

three-cornered straight surgical needle. Tie the
first stitch, then continue up until you reach the
junction of the leg with the body, always, on each
edge of the cut, pushing the needle through from
the skin side; this will draw the stitches down into
the hair so as to be invisible. You will probably
have to renew the thread one or more times on each
leg; always tie your last stitch firmly, and then tie
the first stitch of the new thread. The skin under
the shoulder and hip joints will be loose and must
be tucked up in under as in life and pinned there.
You will now start sewing at the breast and continue
along the cut to the tip of the tail. If your measurements are correctly taken and followed in making the manikin, the skin will fit perfectly everywhere.

If your specimen were any horned animal, you
would have had to also make a cut down the back
of the neck in order to get the skin off over the
horns; in the case of a moose or elk it would also be
necessary to continue this cut down over the back
side of the fore shoulder to meet the cut on the
breast. Thus you will see that a horned animal requires yards more sewing to get the skin on the
manikin, than does the pointer that we illustrate.

Finish up the head by taking the nostrils and lips into place and pinning them; make the eyelids correctly fit the eyes of the manikin, pinning the lids where necessary. Insert clay through the outside opening of the ear to model its junction with the manikin, and bend the ears to their proper shape, those of a pointer of course hanging down as is shown on next page. This figure shows the dog when finished and on a stand. Your specimen at the present stage should look just the same except for the stand. You can drive common pins into the body in any hollows to hold the skin in contact with them, and it is well to wind narrow strips of cotton cloth around the body at the hip and shoulder joints to keep the skin in the proper position during drying; of course this does not apply to any long-haired animals, for the strips would make ridges that could never be effaced.

The specimen should dry thoroughly before placing it on its permanent stand. Then brush it well, comb the hair out smoothly, wax about the eyes, if necessary. With a small brush paint the eyelids dark brown and the muzzle the color of life, which varies from blackish to gray or pink.

Black Bear
Pointer Dog

We advise the mounting of pet animals on finished oak bases, while wild animals look the best on artificial rock or groundwork, direction for making which are given in Chapter 12.

Making Animal Skins

Animals, especially for study purposes, are frequently made into scientific skins instead of being mounted. The animal should be skinned the same as though it were to be mounted.

Poison the skin well; clean and poison the skull and, after wrapping a little cotton about it replace it in the skin. Wrap each leg bone lightly with cotton and turn back. Fill the neck and body of the animal loosely with cotton or excelsior, so as to make the body evenly distended but rather smaller than it was in life. Small animals (no larger than a fox) can have the front legs stretched in front one on either side of the head, and the back ones straight behind. On larger specimens the fore and hind legs are respectively doubled up against the breast and abdomen. No attempt is made to have an animal skin resemble a dead animal. The head may be filled out a trifle through the eyes, and the

Animal skin for the cabinet.

lids left in approximate the correct shape; it is
well to have the body rather flattened than round,
for the skin will then lay in a draw without rolling
all about. Very large skins are simply "baled up"
that is salted well, partially dried and folded and
tied so as to make as small a package as possible.
In such cases the skull is usually kept separately
but of course both skull and skin must be marked.

CHAP. 4--Mounting Heads of Animals

Mounted heads of any of the larger birds or animals make attractive wall decorations and are valuable reminders of the chase. You will often want to do this work for yourself, and many taxidermists derive their chief income from the mounting of deer heads. The methods for mounting animal heads have been, and are, subject to a great many variations. Most of these methods are, however, stuffing, pure and simple, and modern taxidermy does not allow of that. All heads should be modeled, that is the head should be modeled to its true form and have the eyes set before the skin is put on. Most taxidermists continue to use clay for this purpose, but it is far inferior to either plaster or papier-mache, and is used simply because it requires slightly less time and skill. We will describe and illustrate the best method.

Mounting Deer Heads

The instructions that follow apply equally well for mounting any kind of an animal head, large or small.

Before skinning the head, take measurements from the base of the horns to the end of nose, circumference of neck at smallest part and also lower down, at about the point that you decide to cut it off.

Opening cut to skin a deer head.

Skinning—All horned animals must be opened down the back of the neck, and must never be split up the throat. Start from between the horns and make a clean cut down the middle of the neck to the shoulders; thence around the neck both sides, meeting at the base of the fore-neck. This will leave plenty of skin to work with, no matter how long or short you may afterward decide to have the neck on your specimen. Most guides and market-men make the mistake of leaving too little of the neck and the taxidermist is often forced to make his mount fit the skin without regard to its best effect.

From the opening cuts you have made, gradually fold the skin back, cutting it away from the flesh with a keen-edged skinning knife; this work re-

quires a larger and stronger knife than your scalpel
that was used on birds. After having skinned
the neck you will come to the ears. Sever these by
cutting directly through the tissues and cartilage.
Then skin around the base of the horns; this is a
rather tedious process for the novice, but patience
and continued sharpening of the knife will accomplish it. Of course, in order to skin about the horns
you must make a cut from horn to horn, across the
end of your first neck cut. From the horns on, as
the skinning progresses, the scalp is turned inside
out like the taking off of a glove. Care must be
taken in cutting through the membrane of the eye
not to also cut through the lid, which shows through
it as a whitish line. Also use caution just in front
of the eye, where the tear duct is located; the skin
here lies in a hollow in the skull and must be cut
out carefully. The next point to look out for is the
corner of the mouth; here you want to cut through
the skin on the inside of the lip. In cutting through
the nostrils, which you will next meet, keep rather
close to the skull so as to leave enough of the skin
inside the nostrils to well fill it on the mounted
specimen. No further difficulties will be encounter-
ed and the skin is entirely detached from the skull.

Skinned to the
nose.

Albino Maine Deer

Cleaning the Skull

This and cleaning up a scalp or head-skin, are among the most disagreeable pieces of work a taxidermist is called upon to perform, but they must be done and if done with a vim and apparent relish, it will be gotten through with quicker and with most satisfaction. With a meat saw you must saw off the back of the skull, a little back of the horns; you will find that is most convenient to rest the head on the horns and saw through from a point just back of the lower jaws. This exposes the brains which must be scooped out; hold the skull with the cavity downward and this can readily be done with the skinning knife. The eyes must be taken out, first, loosening them around the circumference, then cutting the optic nerves and allowing them to come out whole. Clean all flesh from the skull everywhere, using knife, scissors or fingers, and even a hatchet does not go amiss. Now give the skull a good coat of arsenical soap and put it away to dry, remembering that it must be out of reach of children or any pet animals as it is now dangerous.

Cleaning the Scalp

To do this you will need a pair of heavy scissors, those illustrated in Chapter 10 are the best and most durable. Cut off all flesh or fat that may have been left on the skin. Carefully thin the skin down around the eyes and lips; keep your fingers underneath where you are cutting to keep the skin up firmly against the shears; it will make you more careful too, for if you cut through the skin your fingers are apt to suffer. With your scalpel split down between the inner and outer skins of the nose, and cut all fat and gristle from each.

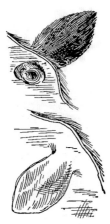

Ear skinned ; turned inside out as in taking off a glove.

Skinning the Ears

All large animals and especially members of the deer family, should have the ears skinned and tinned, otherwise they are almost certain to shrink and warp out of shape at some time, even though they are held firmly in shape during the process of drying.

Ears are skinned by turning them inside out, from the inside of the skin. Start cutting the skin away from the back of the cartilage that fills the ear; you will find that as soon as you have proceeded a little ways you can easily push the skin apart from the cartilage with the finger nails or the wooden handle of your scalpel. The skin on the back of

the ear should be entirely loosened from the cartilage even to the tip.   Rub the ear thoroughly with
salt and turn it back again.

Curing the Scalp

When you have the scalp thoroughly cleaned it
can be cured in either of two ways:—The salt
bath, directions for making which are given in
Chap 10.   This will keep a skin that is immersed
in it, indefinitely and in a soft condition.   For our
work we prefer thorough salting of the skin, using
fine table salt and rubbing it into all parts of the
skin; let the skin lay flat for twenty-four hours,
then pour off water that has accumulated and salt
again, this time folding it carefully up twice.   It
can then be put away and mounted at any time,
it only requiring to be put in a tub of water over
night, which will bring it out as well as when first
skinned.   Each skin should be tagged, giving the
length of nose and girth about ears and back of
neck.   If your skin is to go in pickle, it is best to
write this with pencil on a flat wooden tag.

Scalp ready to
be poisoned.

Making the Form

The first piece to get out is the pear-shaped neck
board.   This is to set in the back of the neck on
an angle and should consequently be a couple of

inches larger than the circumference of the neck at
this point. For a medium-sized deer taken in the
hunting season, this will usually be just about 24
in., so a neck board of 26 in. would be correct;
these figures are not fixed and you must make your
measurements to correspond to your head. Make
this neck board out of inch pine board. The neck
piece is made of two pieces of this board, about
four inches wide, nailed together; the shield end
should be cut on about an angle of 45 degrees. The
length of this piece will depend upon how long a
neck you want on your specimen. A medium length
is the best and the neck piece usually averages
about 12 in. long, measured along the top (this is
the shortest side). The back of the skull is chop-
ped out with a hatchet to accommodate the end of
this neck piece, and the top end of the latter is
rounded a little to fit the shape of the skull. The
sketches show both these neck pieces and the
method of attaching the skull. The skull should be
nailed to the neck so that when placed upon the wall
the bottom of the under jaw will slant slightly
downward.

You will notice in the plate on page 150, that the
nose of the skull has been cut off just in front of

the teeth, and that there is no lower jaw. This
method saves time, both in cleaning and mounting,
for the professional who has many heads to mount
but is not necessary or advisable for the amateur.
When mounting in this way we have a mould and
make a plaster cast to replace the end cut off. The
mould is made from a model and casts from the
same mould used on all deer heads, shaving them
down slightly for very small heads. Unless you are
going to mount a great many herds it will be best
for you to leave the skull entire and build up the
nose on it. The neck is formed of excelsior and
tightly and smoothly wound with string, keeping
the desired form always in mind and being sure
that both sides are even (that one does not bulge
where the other hollows). The plate shows the form
ready to receive its final coating, and this may con-
sist of plaster, papier-mache or even clay, but we
do not recommend the latter.

Framework for
mounting a
deer head.

The one that we illustrate is made with plaster;
if you prefer papier-mache, the operations will be
the same; directions for making this material are
given in Chapter 10. We describe the plaster
method because we believe it to be a little more simple for the novice to master. The only advantage

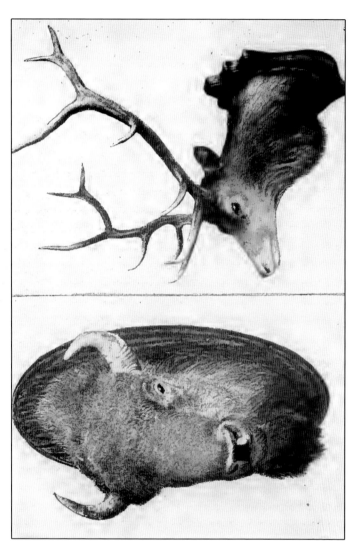

Elk

Buffalo

in the use of papier-mache is in lightness, which
amounts to little after your specimen is done and
on the wall, and is more apt to shrink or warp under
weather changes.

For use, plaster-of-paris is mixed to about the
consistency of cream, with water. It hardens very
quickly, so must be worked rapidly. We advise not
mixing more than a pint at a time until you are used
to working it. Apply with a putty knife or wooden
paddle, evenly and smoothly covering the whole
neck. You will have to mix several lots before your
work is completed, so quickly does it harden.

Wound with
excelsior.

Model the nose to as nearly the size and shape
of the original as you can, making allowance for
the thickness of the skin that is to cover it. Have
the eyes in readiness, and put a dab of plaster in
each eye-socket; as soon as it commences to harden set one eye in the center of each socket, being
sure that they both slant the same way and that the
pupils are horizontal. It is a neat piece of work to
get both eyes in exactly the right position. Usually
you will have to do one of them over several times,
until you get used to it. As soon as you have both
eyes firmly and evenly planted, you can add a

touch of plaster above each, bringing it down so as to form a lid; also build up all muscles and flesh on the face to about their original form. Remember that the more evenly and smoothly you distribute your plaster the less scraping you will have to do to finish it. A long carving knife will be found very useful for smoothing the plaster and scraping it to proper shape, after it is thoroughly hard. The nostrils, mouth and about the eyes can be whittled into shape with the small blade of an old jack-knife; an opening has to be cut for the nostril into which the skin can be tucked, and the same in regard to the mouth. The cut on page 150 shows a head all finished in plaster and ready to have the scadp put on.

Form covered with papier-mache or plaster.

Re-laxing a Deer Scalp

If it has been pickled in your bath, it will need no relaxing, just simple rinsing in fresh water. If cured with salt, immerse the skin over night in a tub of water, being sure that all parts are held beneath the surface (a heavy board floating on the surface of the water is the best means of keeping a skin entirely under). The next morning it will be limp and can be put into a pail of luke-warm water, rubbing any places that have not become thoroughly soft, before doing so.

After soaking a couple of hours more, squeeze out as much water as you can, spread the skin on your bench and thoroughly apply arsenical soap to the skin side, and it is ready to put on.

Put the skin in position, pull it in place around the horns and take a stitch back of each, to hold the skin in place, using waxed strong twine and a large three-cornered needle. If you prefer, you can make a hole with your awl on each edge of the skin where it comes together, and wire them together with copper wire. Either method is equally good and we use one about as much as the other. You will need only two stitches, or, at the most, four, since the skin along the back of the neck is to be tacked to the neck-piece, using inch flat-headed wire nails. (This should be tacked about every inch along both edges of the cut). The skin is then drawn evenly down and tacked on the edge of the neck board at intervals of about one inch.

Skin sewed between horns and nailed to neck piece and board.

The ears are each to have a piece of sheet tin in them, cut to the shape and a trifle smaller than the ear. This is inserted between the skin on the back of the ear and the cartilage and can be put in place at this time from the outside or, perhaps it will be

Mountain Goat   Lynx

better for the novice, before the skin is put on the
head at all. The nostrils should be tucked in the
cavities made for them and a small wad of cotton
pushed in each to keep the skin in position. The
upper, then the under lips must be tucked into their
recesses and pinned there, using common pins for
the purpose, driving them into the plaster with a
tack hammer. The tear-duct should be in place and
a flat-headed wire nail driven through it into the
skull, the head of the nail drawing the skin down
and keeping it in the cavity in the skull. The eyelids are to be carefully tacked into position and a
great deal of the success of your mount will depend
upon the artistic skill with which you can make
these little finishing touches. With a sharp-edged
skinning knife now cut off the superfluous neck
skin, cutting close to the neck board. The head is
now rested upon its horns and a temporary board
screwed on the back-board. This should be quite a
bit larger than the neck-board and should have a
large hole bored near the top edge so you can hang
the head up to dry.

modelling of the eye.

Side view of nose

front view.

The ear, which is already tinned, should be
bent into shape and held in position by driving a

straight, pointed piece of No. 10 wire through its opening. the plaster, tow and into the neck-piece. The wire is now sharply bent over the upper edge of the ear and pinched so as to hold the ear firmly. The natural position for the ears, that is, the one that makes the best and most life-like mount, is to have their top edge just touching the under side of the horns; this throws the ears forward in a very attentive or expectant manner.

Head on temporary board; ears properly wired in position.

Finishing the Head

Your specimen should be allowed to dry for at least a week before doing anything further with it. and longer if your room is cold or damp. Cut off the pins about the mouth as close to the skin as possible, and then, with a nail-set or an inverted nail, drive them in so they will not show. The pins about the eyes should be carefully pulled out with a twisting motion so as not to separate the skin from the eyes. If the lips have been properly tucked in, the mouth will need no further attention. Remove the cotton from the nostrils and smooth up the cavity, if it needs it, with a little melted wax. Wax should also be used to fill any crack that may show about the eyes. Brush the head up well, comb the hair on the neck, and it is ready to be put on its shield.

The shape of the shield and the material of which it is made are entirely matters for individual taste. Sketches on page 139 show some common and artistic forms that are used. Your dealer in supplies can probably furnish you with shields or you can have a cabinet maker make up your own design.

Having the head on the shield, it remains but to paint the eyelids and tear-ducts dark brown and the muzzle black, when your work will be entirely completed. These directions may appear to be lengthy and to, at first glance, give one the idea that mounting a head is a very difficult piece of work. The contrary is the case; it is easily done, but we believe that explicit instructions are better than too meagre ones, and so have explained everything as fully as possible. As a matter of fact, anyone, by working his brains a bit, can go ahead and mount a very successful deer head by the aid of these accompanying illustrations alone.

Profile of a well-formed head.

head turned to one side.

Mounting Other Heads

The foregoing instructions are adapted without change for mounting elk, moose, coribou, antelope, or any member of the deer family.

Fur-bearing animals, such as bears, dogs, cats, etc., should have the hair thoroughly dried out in sawdust before mounting. The Rocky Mountain Goat is the only hair-bearing American animal that requires drying of the hair before mounting.

This animal has fine, pure white hair and should be washed in soap and water, given a naptha bath and then dried by rapidly dusting dry plaster through the hair. The forms for all animal heads are made the same,—out of wood, skull and plaster, or papier-mache.

Frame for mounting Lynx head.

ready for the scalp.

Open Mouths

The head is mounted as already explained but of course we must make an artificial tongue. This is whittled to as true a shape as possible out of wood and then waxed. The wax should be melted and a little color added, either oil paint or dry powder will do. It will then give the tongue a very natural appearance. Fasten the tongue in place with wax also.

Bird Heads

These should have a wire firmly attached to the skull when the skin is turned inside out, and the neck wound with cotton. Draw the wire down and attach firmly to the shield and the neck feathers will spread out and form an attractive finish.

CHAP. 5--Tanning Skins

Every taxidermist has to know how to make rugs, tan skins for boas, muffs, etc. For home decoration, where one fox is mounted probably twenty will be made into rugs and the proportion of larger animals is even greater. The tanning of bear, dear and coon skins by hand is a laborious undertaking, but it can be done and done well. However we should advise anyone having large work to send it to a professional tanner, who has the proper machinery for breaking up the fibre.

We will first describe the tanning of a fox skin and the making it into a rug. Other animals are done in just the same way, the only difference being in the amount of work necessary to make the skin soft and pliable.

Shapes for shields

Preparing a Skin for Tanning

Your fox may be freshly killed or, as most often happens, it may be sent to you skinned and dried. In the latter case, it should be split up the middle of the belly to the chin, and across on the inside of each foreleg to the toes. Then immerse it, tail and

Mastiff
St. Bernard

all, in luke-warm soapy water and leave over night. In the morning it will be thoroughly relaxed, and should be squeezed out and thoroughly dried in sawdust.

If your fox is in the flesh, make a cut from the chin to the root of the tail, and down the middle of each leg to the toes; remove the skin and clean off all flesh or fat, either with the fingers or scissors. It will then be ready for stretching.

Papier-mache half head for a fox.

A skin for a rug may have the head mounted with an open mouth, showing teeth and tongue; it may be mounted with a half head, mouth closed; or it may be left flat with no eyes in. If the head is to be mounted at all it should be done before the skin is stretched.

Wild Cat.

Mounting the Head

You can either use the natural skull or an entirely artificial head. Your dealer in naturalist's supplies will carry in stock, papier-mache heads of either the half-head or open-mouth variety, and for most any kind of an animal.

Open mouth head for a fox rug.

If you wish to make the head yourself, clean the skull well, and dry it with the jaws set in the position you wish; it is advisable not to have the mouth very wide open. When the skull is well dried you can cover it with papier-mache, to replace the flesh and muscles that formerly covered it. We would advise that you put the eyes in the head as you model it. Remember the excellence of your completed work depends wholly upon the correctness of form and symmetry that you give to this model. If you wish to make the rug with a half-head the skull would be not only useless but a hindrance. The half-head that your dealer can furnish will be much better for this purpose than any you could make, unless you went to the trouble of making a mould and making the heads of paper, as he does.

With the head all made and dry, it is a simple matter to place the skin on it and pin in position. It is best to use short pins around the mouth and to drive them way in, the hair covering the heads. When using a ready-made head, you will usually have to fill in a trifle over the eyes with cotton, and, of course, the glass eyes will have to be set in, in putty, after you have the skin tacked on.

Opening Fox for a rug.

Stretching Skins for Rugs

For this purpose you will need a stretching board about three by four feet. You can make this by cleating boards together or you can use the side of a large box. The board must be in a horizontal position when the skin is tanning, so do not figure on using the side of the barn for stretching board. Lay the skin down on this board, hair side down, and if the head is mounted let it project beyond the board so as not to flatten the ears. Drive a nail or wire through the back end of the mounted head so as to hold it to the board in such a way that its bottom will be about on the same plane as the surface of the board. Next draw the base of the tail down as far as possible without unduly stretching the skin, and nail through the skin.

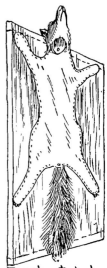

Fox skin tacked on board for tanning.

The skin should be tacked to the board about every inch around the edge; one inch flat-headed wire nails are the best for the purpose. Stretch points on opposite sides of the skin at the same time so that you may get it even.

Pour tanning liquor (receipt for which is given in Chapter 10) on the skin in small quantities, rubbing it in with a wad of tow or excelsior until the

American Magpie

skin is well wetted with it. Then put the board
away and allow the skin to dry. The skin will turn
white under the influence of the tanning liquor,
which eats into the fibre so as to make it break up
readily. The following day or at least in two days
the skin should be dry.

A single application of the liquor is usually
enough for a fox skin, while a dog, coon or larger
animal may require two or even three applications,
letting the skin dry between each, and rubbing it
with some blunt ended instrument, such as the
square end of a file or even the end of a stick of
wood.

The skin can now be removed from the board and
the edges be trimmed with a sharp scalpel. By
brisk and continued rubbing of all parts of the
skin between the hands, the fibre may all be broken
and the skin made very soft and pliable. The
longer it is rubbed the better the tan will be, although fifteen or twenty minutes should suffice for
a fox skin that has been properly treated.

Skull of Fox.

Skull covered wit'
papier mache;
eyes set in.

Tongue of wood
to be finished
with wax.

Lining the Skin

After the skin has been made pliable it can be

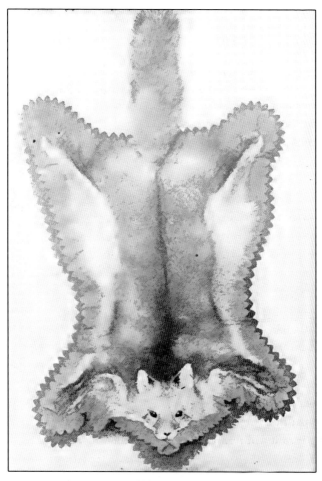

Fox Rug
(Mounted with a half head and lined with two rows of felt)

lined to suit the taste. Rugs are usually lined with
two rows of felt, having the edges "Pinked." Skins
the size of a fox or small dog usually are entirely
lined with felt, while larger ones may have the un-
derpart of the skin covered with denim and two
rows of felt outside of this. The color of felt to
use must suit your own taste; as a rule it is best to
have the inner row of felt a similar color to the
skin as it gives the rug a larger appearance. For
foxes we usually use black and old gold, or an olive
green and old gold, the gold coming next to the
hair.

Felt "pinked" and
stitched

Skin sewed on.

For the outer piece of felt, you will need a piece
about eight inches larger than the skin is, exclusive
of the tail, which is not lined unless it has to be
split in the skinning.

Lay the skin on this piece of felt and with a
piece of chalk mark around it about four inches
from the skin. Cut the inside color into four inch
strips; these are pinned to the other pieces, gather-
ing it so it will turn all corners, and allowing about
two inches of the lower felt to show. It is then
stitched together either on the machine or by hand.
The skin is now sewed on with strong linen thread,

sewing over and over all around the edge. Make
awl holes in the edge of the head at several points
where it touches the felt and sew through these.

The iron to "pink" the felt can be obtained at
any hardware dealer's. The felt is laid on the end
of a smooth block (a chopping block will do) and
the iron tapped through it with a hammer. Of
course this is to be done before the felts are sewed

Pinking Iron.

together. Irons can be had to produce various
shapes, but the one we illustrate on this page is
most commonly used and most satisfactory. One
that makes a scallop an inch wide will be the most
serviceable. A machine can be had for doing this
pinking, but it is quite expensive and hand work
will suffice unless you are going to make rugs by
the hundred.

The tanning of deer, bear skins, etc., can be done
with this same liquor, but it is hard work and no
taxidermist would want to undertake it for the
price that he can get it done at a tanner's.

Such skins have to be pared and shaved down
fairly thin with a tanner's knife (or a sharp draw-
shave will answer), before stretching and applying
the liquor.

Tanning Skins Whole

If a skin is to be used for a boa or is simply to be hung up for decoration, it is best not to slit it down the belly; the cut should be made across the abdomen and down each hind leg, the skin then readily turning inside out, from off the whole body. Skins to be tanned this way should have a board (for a fox about six inches wide and three feet long) with a slightly tapering end, inserted inside the skin while it is skin side out, and then draw the skin down to make it as long as possible and tack to the board at the root of the tail. It is then tanned the same as before.

A fox tail, on a rug, should have a string run through it and knotted at the end.

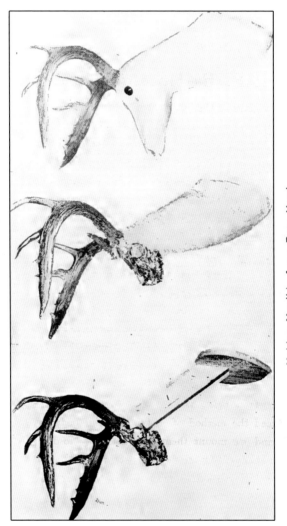

Making Manikin for a Deer Head

CHAP. 6--Mounting Fish

In the days of the "old school" of taxidermy, fish were regarded as the most difficult objects to "stuff." In the present day, most of the difficulties have been overcome, but still a fish represents one of the "nicest" pieces of work that a taxidermist can undertake. A bird has its feathers and an animal its hair to hide defects in the making of the body, but the skin of a fish will only serve to magnify them. Years ago, fish were "stuffed" with tow and then sewed up; after that they were sewed up and filled with sand through the mouth (we have seen some very fair fish mounted by this method too); the next step was forming a body of two and covering it with clay. This method is largely used to-day, but the results obtained by most taxidermists are only awkward caricatures of the original, and far, far, from being satisfactory. In 1885 we first introduced the method of making a solid body of wood, and we mount them the same way to-day, without change. Other taxidermists are gradually adopting this method, which is really the only one that has ever been wholly satisfactory.

Caring For and Preserving Fish

It frequently happens that you will see or catch a fish that you would like to mount, yet you may be far from your headquarters. You can preserve the fish entire, for an indefinite period, but putting it in a jar containing either an alcohol or formaldehyde bath. Directions for making both of these are given under their headings in Chapter 10.

If you make an accurate life-sized drawing of the fish, you can skin it and preserve the skin either by salt or in the same alcohol bath. It is much better, however, to keep the fish wet until after it is mounted.

Skinning a Fish

There are two methods of exhibiting fish,— fastened on panels, showing one side only, or elevated on a standard by means of two upright rods, showing either side. We think the former is by far the preferable. Both sides of a fish are exactly alike; one mounted on a panel occupies less space than if on a standard; and the opening cut does not show, for no one is so expert that he can cover it so it cannot be seen. In either case the fish is skin-

ned the same way, the only difference being that to
mount on standards the opening cut is made on the
belly, from the tail to the point of the lower jaw.
We will describe and illustrate the panel method.

Remember to always keep a fish wet while you
are working upon it. Put a wet cloth on your bench
and have a bowl of water and a piece of cotton with
which to keep moistening the fins, tail and scales.

The fins tear easily when drying and the scales
fall out only too readily, so we must exercise every
precaution to prevent this.

You will need no sawdust or meal when skinning
a fish; just water. Select the best side of your fish,
the one that has the least blemishes, for the front
and lay it on the bench with that side down. A
little above the middle of the side on nearly every
species of fish, you will notice what is called the
median line; on some fish it really looks as though
the skin were stitched together along this line. The
opening cut is made along this line from the gills
to the root of the tail. You will find that you can
do this most easily with the scissors, by inserting
one point under the skin and cutting along the line.

A trout is the easiest and most satisfactory fish to

Dotted line shows
opening cut

Ruffed Grouse   Brook Trout

(Mounted under oval convex glass)

mount, so we would advise you to try your skill
on one of these.

As a rule those fish are the easiest to mount that
have the smallest scales, because the loss of a few
scales is less noticeable, and this loss is very difficult to repair on any fish.

Lift the skin up along the cut, a little at a time,
pushing or cutting the flesh away from it.

On some fish the flesh separates from the skin
easily while on others it has to be cut away all over
the whole body. With the scissors, you will have to
cut through bony edge of the skin back of the
gills, from the point where the median line meets it
to the apex under the lower jaw; then continue
down around the bony edge until you meet the median line on the opposite side of the fish (the front
side). As you skin down the side of the fish towards the belly the first obstruction you meet is
one of the pectoral fins, those that are on the side
of the fish nearest its head. Insert the scissors under this and cut it off. Do the same with the ventral fins, the two that are located side by side about
midway of the belly of the fish. The next fin that

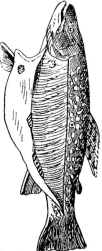

Pectoral fin cut
off and roots of
Anal and Ventral exposed.

you will strike on the belly side of the fish is the
anal (the large one near the tail); cut its bony
connecting links as close to the skin as possible, using care not to cut through the skin. Do the same
on the back of the fish with what is called the dorsal
fin.

You now have one-half the skin on the fish clear
from the body, and we trust that you have not forgotten to keep the whole skin and fins wet during
this time. Cut through the bony root of the tail until you come to the skin on the other side, taking
care not to cut through that.

You now turn the fish over, with its body resting
on the cloth and the loosened skin spread on either
side. Lift the tail up and gradually work the flesh
away, turning the skin carefully back so as not to
disturb the scales, until you reach the head.

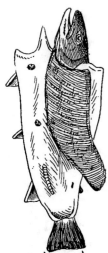

Body loosened
from the skin up
to the head.

With your large scissors cut right through the
backbone (inside the skin of course), just back of
the head; the body will then be free from the skin.
Cleaning out the head is a slow undertaking. It
has to all be cut out with the scissors; by keeping as
closely to the skin as possible you will be able to
get out a fairly large chunk, including the eyes and

what little brains a fish has. Most of it, however, will come out in very small pieces; keep at it until you have the upper part or the head fairly clean. You can leave the lower jaw in, but cut out the tongue and scrape away as much flesh as possible. In cleaning the head, look out for the teeth with which most fish are armed; they make severe and painful scratches if you are careless.

Wash out the cloth on which you have been skinning and lay it as smoothly as you can on your bench. Spread the fish skin, skin side up, on it just as smoothly as possible. Hold the skin firmly down with the left hand to prevent slipping and, with the blade of the scalpel, carefully scrape the skin, getting off all particles of flesh or fibre that cling to it. Trim the fin bones off flush with the skin inside. You will find that they can be dislocated on the wooden form; if this is not going to be done at once, put the skin in a jar of water.

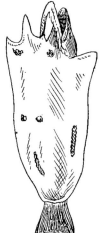

skin cleaned;
ready for body.

Making the Form

If you have a fresh, unskinned fish at your workroom, you should always make the wooden form for

Newfoundland Caribou

its body before skinning the subject. If the fish is
already skinned you will have to make the form
from measurements.

Lay the fish the most perfect side up, on a piece
of paper in the position that you wish to mount it.
Mark carefully around it with a pencil. Cut this
paper out with scissors along the line.

Get a piece of straight-grained soft pine the
length of the fish from nose to root of tail and of a
thickness equal to that of the fish in his largest
part. Place the paper pattern on this block and
mark around it. By holding this block in a vise you
can whittle it into shape with a sharp draw-shave.
The finished specimen should have the tail laying
in the same plane as the back side of the body, so
you will curve the body slightly, being sure that
you curve the right side so as to show the best side
of your specimen in front. We have seen a body
made curved one way and then the fish opened on
the wrong side when skinned; be careful that you
do not get into this fix. The body must correspond
in every respect of form and measurement to the
fish as it lays on your bench. (Remember to keep
the fish on wet cloth). It can be smoothed up with
a spoke-shave and then sandpapered. The head
will want a hollow groove cut in it where the lower
jaw-bone is located and a hole to come beneath the
eye hole in the skin. Give the body a good coat of

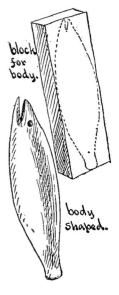

block for body.

body shaped.

white lead paint and let it dry while you are skinning the fish. It will be better if you keep the fish
skin in water and do not mount it until the following day so as to give the paint a chance to harden.

Of course, your paper pattern must be made
without regard to the fins and tail, and your wooden
form is to be devoid of these appendages.

Putting the Skin on Form

Skin tacked on
the body.

You will still need the piece of wet cloth on your
bench, and every few minutes until your fish is
completed, you must wet the fins. Lay the form
on your bench, front side up. Place the skin carefully in position taking care that no flesh or foreign
matter get between the skin and form to cause un-
sightly humps. Rub a little mixed clay on all the
fin joints inside the skin, after having carefully
turned the body over, in the meantime holding the
skin firmly from slipping on it. Draw the edges
of the skin together and they should just meet, if
the body was made just correctly; if they come
within a small fraction of an inch it will be all
right, since the joint is not to show; still the careful workman will always see that it does meet cor-

rectly and there is a great deal of satisfaction in having your work right.

Tack it along both edges of the cut, using ordinary small flat-headed tacks, (if you should have opened your specimen on the belly you will have to tack it with common pins, cutting each off short after you have driven it in a short distance).

Put a thin layer of clay on the inside of the top and cheeks of the head; this is necessary because it is impossible to thoroughly clean all particles from these regions. Pin the apex, at the front of the belly-skin, in position between the gills, and draw these latter into their proper place and pin them there (driving common pins through the bony structure into the wood, and afterwards cutting them off short).

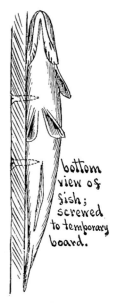

bottom view of fish; screwed to temporary board.

Pin the upper and lower jaws into place, the latter fitting in the hollow made for it in the wooden form. Set the eyes in clay. You will notice that fish have different eyes from any of the birds or animals. The pupil is irregular and the iris often colored with gold or silver. Your dealer will probably have fish eyes in stock; if not you can get the uncolored eyes, having only the pupil and color them yourself.

The pectoral fins of a fish are usually carried at the side or out a little from the body, so the one on

Piping Plover and Young

the back side of your specimen will not show and can be pinned to the side.

Screw a temporary board to the back of the fish; this will serve to protect the fins and to hang it up while drying. The pectoral and ventral fins are held at the proper angle from the body by driving a pin through the base of each into the form. The pectoral, ventral, anal and dorsal fins are spread and held in position with a strip of ising-glass or mica on each side, clamping the two pieces together with wires.

The tail should lay flat against the board; it should be spread and held with a strip of card tacked to the temporary panel. Put your specimen where it will not be disturbed until dry. Fish dry quickly and if the room is of ordinary temperature it should be dry in about two days.

Painting

When the fish is dry, you will find that the colors have nearly all faded, but probably most of the markings will still be faintly visible. This is the best time to paint the subject, for in time even the markings will entirely disappear.

It will be far preferable if, when you are ready to paint the fish, you can obtain a fresh one to refer to, as well as your drawing. At any rate, do not attempt to mount a fish without first making a

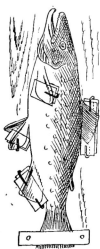

Fins held in place with isinglass and wired.

record of all the colors. You will find that you can carry them in your mind perfectly as long as the specimen stays bright; as he begins to fade, so will his natural appearance from your mind; when his colors have entirely gone, you will find, to your sorrow (if you have no sketch) that your recollection as to its appearance is about as blank as the skin of the fish.

All fish shade from darker on the back to light on the belly. Paint the back and sides of your specimen first, using the colors very thin (use transparent oil paint), so that the fish will not have a "painty" appearance; next put the ground color on the belly and blend it with that of the back and sides. If any of the scales are off, you will have to outline them with a fine brush.

You can now strengthen the markings on the specimen, if it naturally has any, such as stripes or spots. If the head is not perfectly smooth, wax it before painting so as to make it so.

Having completed the painting, you will have to let it dry about two days more; then you can give it a coat of good quality varnish. This will bring out the color and give the glossy appearance a fish has on being pulled from the water.

When the varnish is dry, take the fish from the board, lay it front down on a soft dry cloth; wax the opening cut and paint the back, of course, pay-

ing the most attention to those parts nearest the
top and bottom of the fish, which may show when
it is on its panel. Let it stand until dry.

Finishing

A fish can be displayed to good advantage on
either an oval or rectangular oak panel; or it can
be placed in a hollow box, with painted background and galss front. The best method of displaying a fish for house decoration is to put it under an oval, convex glass, with a painted background and neat frame. This method will be the
most expensive, but it makes a dining-room decoration that cannot be surpassed; a well-mounted and
colored fish is worthy of being so framed.

Mounting Large Fish

Fish not more than three feet in length, we always mount with solid wooden bodies. Fish of
more than that length are best done by making a
wooden center board, winding it with tow or excelsior and covering with either plaster or papier-
mache the same as in making a manikin for a large
animal. This manikin, when dry, should have one
or two coats of white lead, the same as the wooden
one.

Snowy Herone
(With background reproduced from Nature)

CHAP. 7--Reptiles

Most persons have a horror of snakes. This dislike also is common among many taxidermists, a great many of whom will refuse to mount one, either because they do not know how or are afraid to. With few exceptions, snakes are about as harmless creatures as we have. If one will lose sight of the fact that they are just "snakes" he will soon see that there are a great many beautiful species. The mounting of them is difficult but they make a very interesting collection.

Skinning

A snake skins very easily; in fact, it is much easier to skin a snake than it is to kill it. Snakes, that is the majority of them, are useful creatures so do not kill one unless you have use for it, and then do not smash its head with a club or rock. Catch your snake by pinning it to the ground with a stick so that you can grasp it by the neck with the left hand; then kill it by forcing the blade of

King Snake.

your jack-knife into its mouth and severing the backbone just back of the head, taking care not to cut through the skin.

Aside from the use of chloroform, this is the most painless method of killing a reptile; then it will take some minutes before all motion will cease.

A snake sheds its skin by breaking it about the neck and then crawling out; you can skin one in nearly the same manner, by making a short slit on the throat and then drawing the body from the skin, but this method loosens most of the scales on the body and is to be strongly condemned. The only correct way to skin a snake is to split it the entire length of the under side, after which you can lay the skin back and easily remove the body, without the loss of a single scale. The bony structure of the head has to be cut out with the scissors. Poison the skin well with arsenical soap.

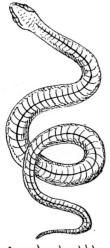

A snake should be opened the entire length underneath.

Mounting

If you have a freshly killed snake it is much better to make the body before you skin the specimen. You can then be certain that it is exactly as it should be. Two wires are used in a snake body, one from the head to the vent and thence out through the skin; this wire is usually the only support needed and should be large enough to sustain the snake in the position that you intend to place it in. The other wire is twisted about this above the vent and continues on down to the end of the tail.

Wind this wire form with tow so as to be slightly smoother than the specimen; wind it firmly and smoothly with the cops and bear in mind that the smoother you get the body the better the finished work will be. It must now be bent to approximately the shape that you wish the snake to occupy. If it is to be coiled, have the coils separated so that you can get at it to sew the skin on; they can then easily be closed together without destroying the shape of the specimen. This tow body must be smoothly covered with either papier-mache or clay.

The snake is then skinned as described above and the skin very carefully put upon the manikin. Of course the excellency of your work will depend entirely upon the body you have made; the skin should just meet the whole length. It must now be sewed up the whole length, a tedious job and one requiring skill and a delicate touch to avoid destroying the contour of the body. You can now fasten the specimen on a temporary board by

Artificial body made of wire wound with tow, covered with clay.

Prong-Horn Antelope

means of the wire which projects from the vent, adjust the coils as you want them and see that the whole body is entirely free from humps or hollows.

The eyes for the specimen will have to have vertical pupils. You can get the proper size of clear glass and color them yourself. They can be set in putty as soon as the specimen is mounted or if you do not happen to have the eyes on hand you can put them in by softening the lids, at any time.

The cut must be carefully sewed the whole length.

When the specimen is dry, the seam on the underside should be waxed wherever it is visible and the specimen, especially if it was a bright colored one will have to be retouched with oil paint for the color fades a great deal on all serpents.

Another Method

The snake can be skinned as before and filled with either sand or fine sawdust. Commencing at the tail, sew up a couple inches, then fill this section with sand, pressing it firmly into a round shape; then sew up a couple inches more and so on until you have the entire specimen filled but not "stuffed" beyond its original proportions. When using this method it is best to bend the body in po-

sition as you fill it, for it is difficult to bend it afterwards without destroying its symmetry. If you
wish, and we think it is the better way, you can
start a wire in the body at the tail and keep it in
the center the whole length.

This gives a great deal of firmness that is often
necessary. We consider the first method to be by
far the best, but have both seen and done very satisfactory work by using either. It is best to mount
your specimen with the mouth closed until you
have become quite expert; it requires a great deal
of artistic talent to successfully model the interior
of a serpent's mouth.

CHAP. 8

Collecting and Mounting Butterflies and Moths

A taxidermist is supposed to, and should, know how to mount anything that may be brought to him.

Few collectors confine themselves to just one branch; they should be familiar with the members of other branches and know what to collect and how to preserve anything they may come across. So a few words relatives to the collecting and mounting of various kinds of insects will not be amiss in this volume.

Butterflies and moths form very beautiful and interesting collections. Of course they are very fragile and, until improvements within recent years, the caring for a collection has been a trying job.

Now with the Denton and Riker mounts, they can be collected with the assurance that they will be safe from the ravages of insects and from breakage.

Collecting

We will not go into extensive discussion of the many methods by which insects can be caught. The

Horned Owl   **Snowy Owl**
(Framed under convex glass with painted backgrounds)

butterfly net is the instrument most often used. The most simple form of net, that of a hoop of wire, covered with muslin or mosquito netting, and attached to the end of a stick is as effective as any and can be made at home by anyone. The hoop should be about a foot in diameter and the net should bag about eighteen inches. Many forms of folding nets have been made. The most serviceable one that we know of is one that is made for a landing net for fishermen. You can find one at a sporting goods house or at many hardware dealers. Of course the fish net has to be removed and a fine net bag substituted. It comes with a short handle which may be replaced with a longer one if desired. This net folds into a package about an inch in diameter and a couple feet long, while when open it is as rigid as a non-folding net. As soon as a fly is caught a slight twist of the wrist will fold the bag over the frame so as to imprison the insect in the lower end.

Butterfly net

folded.

Of course the most perfect flies are those raised from cocoons or chrysalids; these can often be found on the ground or hanging to branches or rails. Often you can get the worms or caterpillars and by feeding them upon the leaves upon which you find them, they will usually transform themselves into either cocoons or chrysalids from which the moth or butterfly will later emerge.

Bright lights attract most moths and the most fruitful places in which to find these are about arc lights on the outskirts of a city at night.

Killing Insects

Pinned on board, top down.

All butterflies can readily be killed by compressing the body, between the thumb and fore-finger, directly under the wings; if care is used their feathers will not be injured in the least. They can be pinched right through the net before removing. Moths have large bodies and if treated in the same way the juices would soil them. These are best killed with a drop of naptha or benzine on the head. This is also used for killing any kinds of bugs. Any specimen should be mounted as soon as possible after killing with naptha for it hardens the joints much quicker than if they are killed in other ways. Many kill their specimens by putting them in a cyanide jar. The making and use of this is described under the head of cyanide in Chapter 10.

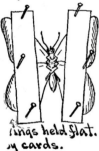

Wings held flat. by cards.

Mounting

With the mounts that are now used for displaying flies, it is unnecessary to have the setting boards with a groove for the insect's body, such as were formerly used. Tack a piece of card to a smooth board; spread the wings of the fly and lay it, top down, on this. Pin through the center of the body into the board and stretch each wing into the proper position and pin it (with one pin close to the body).

In a correctly mounted, fully-spread fly the lower edge of the upper wings should form a straight line across on either side of the body. All insects for a collection should be mounted in this way. When you have the wings spread, pin a strip of card across both the upper and lower ones.

Compressing lungs.

A drop of naptha on the head kills moths quickly.

Killing insects.

The pin in the body may now be carefully drawn out and the antennæ must be pinned evenly in front of the head. They will dry and be ready to put in the mount in a couple days.

The Riker mount is composed of cotton in a box, with a glass cover. The fly is laid on the cotton and the cover put on, this pressing the specimen firmly into the cotton and protecting it from moths or breakage. A folded fly may be put in the same mount with a spread one to show both the upper and under sides; the chrysalids and mounted caterpillars as well as the pressed plants that they feed upon are often also included, thus giving a life history of the species. These mounts lend themselves readily to many decorative effects for wall ornaments, by combining pressed flowers with bright colored butterflies.

The Denton mount is made of plaster, with a depression in the center for the insect's body.

Riker Mount.

The fly is put in position with a touch of glue under each wing and the cover glass put on and bound with paper. Another Denton mount has glass both front and back to show both sides of a fly. This is an excellent one for scientific study of the insect.

Caterpillars and Worms can be mounted as follows:

Squeeze the insides entirely out through the anus. It will probably require some practice before you can be sure of doing this successfully.

Denton Mount.

Insert the end of a straw or small tube in this opening and expand the skin with the breath, at the same time holding it above heat (a lamp will do) and continually turning it so it will dry evenly and in the proper position. Take care not to stretch the skin or to get it near enough to the heat to scorch it. The tube may be either cut off short or removed. Many bright colored specimens will have to be retouched with oil paint as the colors are very apt to leave.

CHAP. 9

Collecting and Preparing Eggs

Only a very few years ago the collecting of bird eggs was a very common thing; scarcely a boy but had a small collection. Fortunately this has been discouraged as well as prohibited by law, so that at present it is necessary to have a permit from the state to collect and then only for scientific purposes. Unless our reader intends to make Ornithology or Oology a special and permanent study, we entreat him not to start a collection of eggs.

Such collecting is permissible and may be beneficial to science if properly and conscientiously carried out.

In some parts of the country birds can be found nesting at all seasons of the year, but, as a rule, the nesting season occurs in the months of May, June and July.

For collecting eggs in the field, a small satchel, a fish basket or even a dinner box swung over the

Wood Duck
(The most beautiful of all ducks)

shoulder with a strap, are the best receptacles. Each egg must be snugly wrapped in cotton and carefully put away in the box.

Single eggs are worthless; they must be collected in whole, original sets and usually the nest should be taken along with them. One of the worst practices that ever prevailed was the taking of a single egg from a nest. Nine out of ten of our wild birds will immediately leave a nest if a single egg is taken.

Eggs must be blown with but a single hole, and that in the side, otherwise they are of no value. Drills made expressly for this purpose may be obtained of your dealer in supplies. They have fine machine-cut burs on the head, which when the drill is rotated between the fingers, rapidly cuts a round hole in the side of an egg. An egg shell is very fragile and the drill must be handled with the greatest of care. Sometimes it is best to start the hole with the point of a small pin. The contents of the egg are easily removed by forcing air through this hole with a blowpipe. The end of the pipe must never be inserted in the egg. Simply blow the air through it, with the mouth, into the

opening and the contents will come out the same
hole. We consider that any form of water or hand
blower is useless. Eggs must not be collected in
any quantity sufficient to make a water blower
necessary and for a small number of eggs at a time,
your own bellows are far better than any artificial
ones.

Blowing an egg.

Sometimes eggs will be collected, that have well
formed young in them. Of course, unless it should
be some rare species, they should not be taken unless they are believed to be fresh. By using care
a good sized chick can be removed without damage
to the shell if you have embryo scissors and a hook
with which to cut it up. After you have the contents cleaned out of the egg, blow a mouthful of
water in to rinse it out. Wipe it carefully with a
soft cloth and the egg is ready to be marked for
the cabinet.

Marking an egg.

Of course an egg the identity of whose parents
is unknown, is useless; so never take a set unless
you know what it is, or secure the bird to identify
it by.

Eggs are marked with a soft black pencil; each
egg has to have the A. O. U. No. of the bird, fol-

lowed by the set number. Suppose you find one
set of 3 Blue Jays and two sets of 4 eggs each.
The first set would be marked 477 1-3, the second 477 1-4 and the third 477 2-4. Each egg of a
set must be numbered with the same set mark. A
good form of data blank is shown in the marginal
sketch on this page. Each set of eggs must be
accompanied by a data such as this. Every set
of eggs collected should be entered on your register
of specimens collected and given its consecutive
number on the data blank just after the heading
"Remarks" which is intended for the composition
and position of the nest. This register of specimens should be in one book or set of books and
every specimen you collect should be entered under a consecutive number regardless of whether it is
beast, bird, fish or egg.

Good form for
a data blank.

The matter of style of cabinet in which to keep a
collection of eggs depends upon individual taste
and the amount of money you can put into it. Most
collections are in cases of shallow drawers, each
set being in a pasteboard tray, which also contains
the data, neatly folded. These trays are of different sizes but all of a uniform depth, 3-4 in.

The following sizes are most often used and they are such that they will fit uniformly into the drawers, each size occupying just twice the space of the size next smaller: 1 1-2 x 2; 2 x 3; 3 x 4; and 4 x 6; these sizes will accommodate most any set. The eggs are safest laid in these trays with no cotton packing whatever.

Tray for eggs

A better but more expensive method of exhibiting an egg collection is to have them in trays about two inches deep and with a cover having a glass top. The eggs are set lightly in cotton and the glass holds them firmly in place; they can be handled by anyone without danger of breakage.

Glass-topped box.

The best method, and also the most costly, is to have the glass-topped pasteboard boxes large enough to take in both the nest and eggs. This of course calls for large boxes and very large cabinets. This last method is the one adopted in the museum of Mr. J. E. Thayer, at Lancaster, Mass., whose collection is one of the finest and most complete in the country.

Box for nest.

CHAP. 10
Tools and Materials Used by the Taxidermist

HOW TO MAKE, OR WHERE TO OBTAIN THEM. HOW TO USE THEM

We do not want you to think that *all* of these following articles are absolutely essential to the taxidermist. Until you get to be an expert you can get along with a very few of them.

We have endeavored to list in alphabetical order practically all the things that any taxidermist will ever wish. Any materials mentioned in the text will be found here, telling where to get them or how to make them, and how to use them.

Alcohol

This is the chief ingredient of shellac and is used for thinning the same when it becomes too thick for use.

One of the most important uses for alcohol is

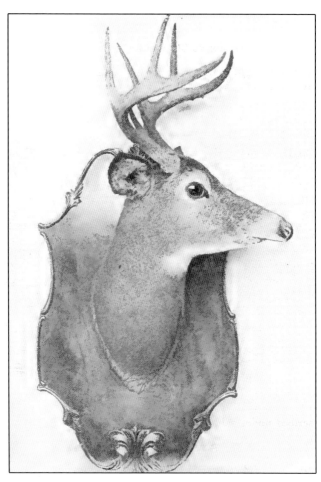

Deer Head
(Turned sharply to left)

the preserving, entire, of small specimens. These may be taken out and mounted at any time, but specimens such as snakes, lizards, fish, etc., are frequently preserved for exhibition in alcohol.

Many druggists sell adulterated alcohol; it should contain at least 94% of absolute alcohol which is recognized as pure. For use the alcohol should be diluted with one-third its bulk of water.

It is best to put it in large-mouthed glass jars, just a bit larger than your specimens require. Whatever the specimen you wish to preserve, it is best to first make a deep cut on the abdomen so the liquid will have free action on their interior.

You can get alcohol at druggists and often at paint stores, but you want *grain alcohol* and not wood, such as dealers in paints most often use.

Alum

Powdered alum is often used by the taxidermist. It is a hardening substance, that is, it will cause the skin of an animal to shrink and harden. It is used chiefly in the "salt and alum" bath, which is described under salt.

Arsenic

By this we do not mean the mineral arsenic, but the white powdered form (arsenious acid). This very necessary article is *Poisonous,* taken internal-

ly or if it gets in cuts or scratches, so it must always be handled with due caution and never left where anyone else can get hold of it; it should always be plainly marked *Poison*. Its fumes are harmless and we know of no case of poisoning except through gross negligence of ordinary precautions. It can be rubbed on the inside of a bird or animal skin in its dry form, but we advise its use in the form of *Arsenical Soap*. You can buy this already prepared of your dealer in taxidermists' supplies or you can make it as follows: Slice two pound bars of white soap into two quarts of water and boil until the soap is melted. Add two pounds of powdered arsenic and four ounces of camphor, stirring the mass to prevent its burning. Add water to make it the consistency of cream, then allow it to cool, stirring it occasionally to prevent the arsenic from settling. Apply it with an ordinary, round stiff-bristled paint brush to any skin that you wish to poison. An agate pail is the best in which to make the soap; do not use any of the family cooking utensils. Keep it in cans, plainly labelled. *Hard Soap* is often used if you are to make an extended trip. It is made just as before but is not thinned, so when it cools it will be about the consistency of butter. This should be kept in tin boxes. It can be used by wetting the brush and working the soap into a lather.

Arsenic Solution

This solution is often used to dip animal skins into, to make them insect proof.

It is made by placing 2 pounds of crystallized arsenic and 1 pound of Bicarbonate of Soda in 4 quarts of water and boiling until the ingredients have thoroughly dissolved. This solution should be kept in a tight bottle and for use be diluted with four times its bulk of water. The skin may be entirely immersed in it or the solution may be sprayed on the fur with an atomizer. This solution answers the purpose very well, but we prefer either Corrosive Sublimate or a Sulphuric Acid solution as described under these heads.

Blowpipe

This is used for blowing bird eggs. It is a brass tube with the end drawn out to a fine point and slightly up-turned. The point is not to be inserted in the hole in the egg, but held close to it, forcing the air in, which in turn, forces the contents out. You can obtain this from a naturalists' supply dealer.

Bone Shears

These are large strong scissors capable of cutting through wing and leg bones of large birds.

Brain Spoon

This is a metal rod with the end forged into a
small scoop. It is used for removing brains from
the heads of birds or animals. A great many taxidermists use this instrument but we have always
failed to see any superiority in it over the blade of
the scalpel or points of the scissors, and we certainly would not advise having any additional tools unless there is some distinct advantage to be gained
therefrom. Your supply dealer will have them if
you wish to try one.

Chain and Hooks

This is an article that most books advise and that
some taxidermists use. It is composed of three
stout hooks (not barbed) each attached by a chain
to a ring. They are used to suspend the bodies of
partly skinned specimens for the purpose of assist-
ing in the operation.

A block and tackle with a good stout hook is
useful when skinning large animals that are too
heavy to handle, but there are no birds in this
country but what we should prefer to skin without
the aid of a chain and hooks.

When using this contrivance on birds, one hook
is to go through the small of the back after you
have skinned that far; then when you reach the

wings the other two are brought into play. Your
supply dealer can furnish them.

Clay

Potter's clay is always a very useful and often
a necessary article for a taxidermist to have in
stock. Many use it for modelling the faces of animals and for reproducing muscles on the body and
legs (for this purpose, in the majority of cases,
either plaster or papier-mache are preferable)
while for the mounting of reptiles it is indispen-
sible. Clay comes in dry lumps and is heavy, so if
you have to order it from a distance it is best to
get a quantity and have it come by freight. Your
supply dealer will have it, or if there is an iron
foundry near, you can get it there. For use, clay
is either broken up finely with a hammer or rolled
out with a wooden roll.

Water is added in small quantities and mixed
until the clay becomes stiff, so it can be worked
and moulded with the hands. It is best to cut up a
small quantity of tow, as finely as possible and stir
this in with the clay. This adds much to the
strength of the clay when it is dry.

Cops

For winding the plumage of birds as well as for
winding the bodies, nothing is as good as cops.
This is fine, soft, cotton thread that is used for

Pair of Mallards
(Under convex glass)

Sanderling
(With painted background)

spinning in cotton mills. It is so fine that enormous
quantities are wound on a small paper core. It
should have a wire hooked into the projecting end
of the paper core, and be suspended from the ceiling over your work bench. Your dealer in supplies
has these.

Cork Bark

This is a thick, but light, bark of a South American tree. It is very useful in both commercial and
ornamental taxidermy, for the making of artificial
stumps. It comes in pieces up to as large as eight
or nine inches in diameter and three or four feet
long. Your supply dealer will have it.

Corn Meal

Unbolted corn meal may be used in places of
sawdust for taking up moisture when skinning specimens. It is necessary to use this if the flesh is to
be saved for eating, because it washes off easily
while sawdust sticks. Sawdust is much the best
though for specimens whose meat is not to be saved. Every grocery store keeps it.

Corrosive Sublimate
(Bicloride of Mercury)

This is a poison, a solution of which is used for
preventing the destruction of specimens by insect

Cork bark.

pests. To a pint of alcohol is added one ounce of corrosive sublimate (which is a white powder); shake it and then allow to stand for a couple hours. The powder will not entirely dissolve but you will have the liquid above it fully saturated with the poison. Carefully pour this liquid off into another jar with an equal quantity of water. A skin may be immersed in the liquid and then dried or it may be sprayed on with an atomizer. Some taxidermists keep a metal-lined box filled with fine white sand saturated with this solution, and bury their skins to be poisoned in this box for twenty-four hours. Moths will not touch a skin so treated.

Cotton

This is one of the necessities for the taxidermist. It is used almost exclusively for the filling, in making up skins, and for winding the artificial necks of most birds. Ordinary cotton batting such as all dry goods stores sell is the best for this purpose, and will answer all the requirements of the taxidermist. Absorbent cotton is the best for putting in the mouths of freshly killed birds and for stopping up shot holes, but it is much more expensive than the ordinary and the latter will do.

Cyanide of Potash

Is used in the making of cyanide jars for the

killing of moths and butterflies. You should have a wide-mouthed jar, preferably one with a ground glass stopper for it is necessary to keep the jar closely stoppered when not in use. Place a layer of the crystals in the bottom of the jar and cover them lightly with cotton. Cut a piece of card the size of the inside of the jar, and prick it full of pinholes, push it down on the cotton and fasten with four pieces of gummed paper at equal distances around the edge. A butterfly or moth placed in this jar succumbs in a few minutes, and then should be transferred to the collecting box.

Egg Drill

For drilling holes in birds eggs preparatory to blowing them. These, with fine machine-cut burr, can be procured from your supply dealer. Eggs are blown through one hole in the side, and that hole should be as small as possible.

Embryo Hook

Used for tearing to pieces and pulling embryos from bird eggs. An instrument with a fine hooked point.

Embryo Scissors

Very small scissors, being slender where the two parts cross, so they will work inside of small eggs.

Pileated Woodpeckers
(One of the largest of the species)

Of course the hole is drilled much larger when a chick is in the egg.

Excelsior

Used for the filling of mounted specimens more than any other material. You should get the finest possible, especially for small work.

You can get it of your supply dealer, at furniture stores, mattress makers, at many grocers or in fact any merchant who has goods packed in it.

Eyes

See Chapter 11 for sizes and styles of eyes to use for birds, animals, etc.

Forceps

See tweezers.

Formaldehyde

A five per cent. solution of this (one part formaldehyde to twenty of water) makes an excellent bath for preserving specimens in the flesh. It is equally as good as alcohol and costs but a fraction as much. You can get it at the druggists.

A home-made Glue-pot.

Glue

Glue has no end of uses for the taxidermist, chief of which is probably in the making of stands and rockwork for finished specimens. Prepared liquid glue is all right for putting feathers in birds or patches of hair on animals that need repairing, but pulverized glue is much the best for making bases. You can produce it of any dealer in hardware. It has to be made in a glue-pot or double pail. Two lard pails, one that will go in the other with an inch all around, make an excellent glue-pot. A quart of water and half a pound of glue (or in that proportion) are placed in the small pail and this is set in the large one, which must be half full of water. It must be heated on the stove until the glue melts. It should be of a consistency to run readily but not be watery. It is applied with a stiff-bristle brush.

Glycerine and Carbolic Acid Solution

By means of this solution, specimens after having been skinned can be kept for several months in a soft state, and require little or no further relaxation before mounting. It is very useful for a busy collector on a long field journey as it saves him much time and the skins can be packed flat thus saving a great deal of room.

The solution is made of 2-3 glycerine and 1-3 carbolic acid. It should be thoroughly applied with a soft brush to every part of the inside skin of your specimen. If you are careful you can cover the inside of the skin and get none on the fur or feathers; even if you do no harm is done but you will have to wash it off before mounting. A skin prepared in this way should have a piece of wet cotton placed inside the night before you wish to mount it. The feet should also be immersed for they will become hard.

Grasses

You can get various kinds of dried and colored grasses of your supply dealer. These are used on bases and in making natural surrounding for case work as described in Chapted 12.

Icicles

You can buy these ready made of your supply dealer or you can make them yourself as follows:

Get several pieces of glass tubing, ranging in diameter from 1-4 to 1-2 in. from your druggist. You will need a Bunsen burner (if you have gas in the house, if not an alcohol lamp will do) and a piece of number 14 wire. The latter should be cut into four-inch pieces. Heat the end of one of the tubes and also the end of one of the wires in the flame at the same time. When both are red hot, you can unite them firmly by twisting the wire in the red hot tube; let this cool a bit, then put the tube in the flame again at a point an inch or more from the wire according to the length that you wish to make the icicle; as the glass begins to soften

Heat tube and wire.

Wire welded to glass.

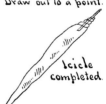

Draw out to a point.

Icicle completed.

pull gently on the wire and the cold end of the tube, and the glass will commence to stretch.

By removing the tube slowly along through the flame, away from the wire, you can draw it down smaller and smaller and finally terminate it by melting the glass entirely off. A little practice will enable you to make these quickly and naturally.

They are attached to branches or rockwork by the wires. See Snow Scenes in Chapter 12.

Leg drill

Vise and needle

Leaves

See under Foliage in Chapter 12.

Leg Drill

This instrument is often useful in making holes in the legs of dried skins so as to allow the wire to pass through when mounting.

You can buy these of your supply dealer or make small sizes out of knitting needles. Get an awl handle at the hardware store; heat one end of the needle red hot, then flatten it on a flat or any iron surface with a hammer. Hold the needle firmly in a vise and drive the awl handle on the flattened end. The other end can be sharply pointed with a file.

Mica Flakes

This is very finely flaked white mica; used commonly in making snow scenes. See Chapter 12. You can get it of your supply dealer.

Moss—See under foliage in Chapter 12.

Naptha
One of the most useful articles for the taxidermist. Used for removing grease from the skins, feathers or fur of specimens before mounting; the best agent for cleaning old mounted birds; for killing moths or dermestes, that may have infected specimens, and for killing butterflies and moths for the entomologist. You can get it at a druggist or a dealer in paints. It is very inflammable and must not be kept or used near a fire or light.

Napthaline Flake
It is well to sprinkle the bottoms of all drawers containing skins with this, as well as to pack it in plentifully with skins, furs or mounted specimens that are boxed for storage. Moths dislike its odor and rarely touch the contents of a box containing it. Druggists keep it.

Needles
Ordinary needles you will of course get from a dealer in dry goods. Three-cornered straight or curved needles are the best for sewing up either birds or animals as the edges of the point cut through the skin much more readily than a round point will. You can get these of your dealer in supplies.

Paint
Many colors and kinds of paints are useful to the professional taxidermist, for coloring bird's feet and bills, fish, and especially for making rock

Needles

Straight 3 cornered

Curved Surgical

Long

Canvas-back Duck
(With natural surroundings)

work and stumps. Anyone can get along very
nicely with the following oil paints which come in
tubes: Chrome yellow medium, chrome green, ivory
black, flake white, vermillion, VanDyke brown,
Prussian blue and burnt sienna. With these colors
you can obtain any shade that you may wish. A
little dab of each color that you wish to use is
squeezed on a clean piece of glass. Dip your brush
into a jar of turpentine and then into the paint.

Papier Mache

Has as many or more uses than any other material used by the taxidermist. It is very inexpensive,
very strong and, when dry, very light. You can
make it as follows: Tear several newspapers into
as small pieces as possible ,and bear in mind that
the cheaper the paper the better pulp it will make;
do not use a glazed paper. Soak these in warm
water for two or three hours then rub the resulting
pulp between the hand until no recognizable pieces
of paper are left. Squeeze it partially dry and
crumble into another dish; add sufficient melted
glue (prepared as described under that head in
this Chapter) to form a very sticky mass when
stirred with a putty knife. Add whiting and work
the mass between the fingers until it becomes
smooth, with absolutely no lumps and only slightly
sticky to the hands. It should be used as soon as
possible after making and you should make no

more than you wish to use for it only keeps a day or two before becoming too hard to work. You can apply it wherever wanted with a putty knife or wooden paddle and shape it with the fingers. It is used for covering skulls for open mouth heads for rug work; covering the skull and neck for mounting deer heads, etc.; repairing broken bills or legs of birds; for rock and stump work. As it dries exceedingly hard it should be left in just the shape and degree of smoothness that you wish before setting the work away to dry.

Pliers

Pinking Iron.

Insect pin

Taxidermist pin.

Pinking Iron

An iron instrument having a sharp-toothed edge for cutting through felt or cloth to make a scalloped edge. Hardware dealers keep them in stock.

Pliers

You can get any size pliers or pinchers that you wish at your hardware dealers. See under Wire Cutters for the best kind.

Pins

While sharpened wires will answer for pinning the wings of any birds, pins are more convenient. For small birds numbers 2 and 6 Insect Pins are the best. (These are longer and more slender than common pins); for large birds Taxidermists Pins can be used. (These are about 2 1-2 inches in length). Either kind can be obtained from your dealer in supplies.

Plaster

Has many uses in the art of taxidermy, chief of which are the covering of manikin for mounted animals and heads, and for drying the plumage of birds. For the first purpose it is mixed with water in sufficient quantity to make it of the consistency of cream, and then applied to the subject with a putty knife as soon as it commences to harden. It hardens within a few minutes and consequently has to be worked very rapidly. You can get it at a dealer in paints, a grain store or often at hardware stores; call for plaster-of-paris.

Putty

Is used chiefly for the setting of the eyes in finished specimens of birds. Get it at a paint store. If it gets too soft, so as to be sticky or oily, add whiting; if it gets too hard to be worked, add boiled oil. Both of these materials you get at the same place.

Sand

You can get mica sand or shell sand of your dealer in supplies. Grits, such as grain dealers keep for chickens, makes a good sand with which to cover bases. When ground fine it imitates granite very well.

Saws

Of course every home or shop should have an ordinary hand saw. A taxidermist should have a meat saw for cutting through skulls of large animals and a hack saw for sawing off iron rods for mounting large animals. If your work is confined to birds you will need only the hand, wood saw.

Salt

Common table salt is used for preserving skins after they have been removed from the animal and well cleaned. If well rubbed with salt and dried they will keep indefinitely and can be mounted at any time.

Salt and Alum Pickling Bath

This bath is used by most taxidermists for picking deer heads and keeping them soft until ready for mounting.

It is made as follows: To every gallon of boiling water add 3 ounces of alum and eight ounces of table salt. Stir until the ingredients are entirely dissolved then allow it to cool and put in large earthen jars, or if you have a large number of skins, in a lead-lined wooden tank. It should be kept covered as it loses its strength if exposed to the air. Skins kept in this will be in condition to mount at any time, even years after they were taken.

Sawdust

This is the best material to use when skinning birds or animals, to take up blood or moisture and prevent soiling of the feathers. Corn meal is best if the specimen is to be eaten, but for other cases it cannot compare with this.

Fine hard-wood sawdust is the best; if you cannot get that any fine quality will do. Get it at any wood-working establishment where they use power saws.

Scalpel

This is the usual surgeons scalpel; a finely tempered blade in a thin ebony handle. It is the best possible knife for skinning small or medium sized specimens. Your dealer in supplies will have them.

Skinning Knife

A much larger knife than the last, used for skinning large animals or cutting off the back of the skulls on birds. Your dealer can furnish you with one.

Scissors

All scissors used by taxidermists should have sharp points on both jaws. A medium sized pair (about 8 in. in length) is suitable for most bird work, and a heavy pair of bone shears is very useful for disjointing and cutting through bones of wings and legs. Your dealer can supply both kinds of best quality steel.

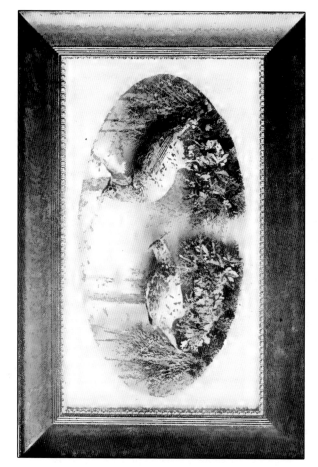

Ruffed Grouse

(Under convex glass; painted background)

Shellac

Is used for painting over stands after they have been sanded. It fixes the sand more firmly in place so it will never fall off. It also brings out the color of paint more strongly and adds gloss if wanted.

Stuffing Forceps

These forceps have very long jaws and scissor handles. They are useful for putting cotton in the necks of long-necked species. One twelve inches long is the most useful. Your supply dealer keeps them.

Tanning Liquors

To make, use: Water, 1 gallon; salt, 2 pounds; alum, 1-2 pound; sulphuric acid, 1 ounce. Mix these thoroughly, adding the acid the last. This acid is poison, and burns clothes as well as flesh so be careful in using it. Keep the liquor in closely stoppered bottles. Its use is explained in Chapter 5.

Tow

Is finer than excelsior and is better for making bodies of small birds and for the necks of large ones. Oakum, on account of its tar odor, which is offensive to insects, is better than the common tow, but costs a trifle more. You can obtain either of your dealer in supplies.

Tweezers

These instruments are indispensable for the taxidermist. A small pair with sharp points is best for picking over and smoothing the plumage of birds. Your dealer can supply you or you can often get them of a hardware dealer.

Wax

This is very useful for finishing about the eyes and mouths of large animals, and on fish and reptiles. The white wax is the best. You can get it of a druggist. For use, melt it in a tin, over a fire or lamp; use a small tin cover and only melt the quantity you wish to use; when melted stir in a dab of paint, the color that you want. The colors most used are black or vermillion and white. You can apply the melted wax with a small stick, wire or brush.

Whiting

Is used for hardening putty that is too soft or sticky; in making papier-mache; for mixing with glue-water to make white for winter scenes; and to rub on skins after having tanned them to make them whiter and softer. Any dealer in paints will have this.

Wire

See Chapter 11 for sizes of wire for different subjects.

Wire Cutters

The best kind of cutters that you can get are Parallel Pliers with cutters attached. These give a double leverage so as to cut wire easily and also are the best pliers made. They have an opening through the handle that will allow a No. 10 wire to pass through, so by using a sharp wire it serves as an excellent leg-drill. Your dealer in supplies or a hardware dealer will keep them.

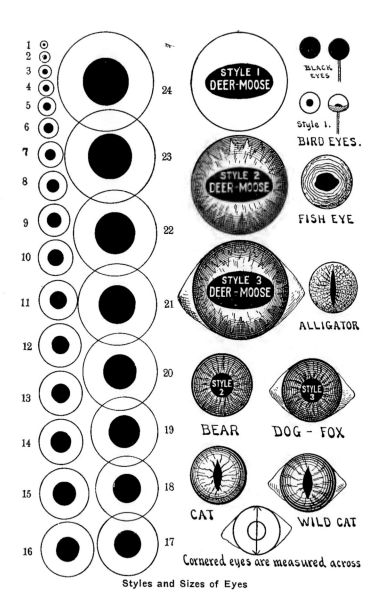

1
2
3
4
5
6
7
8
9
10
11
12
13
14
15
16

24
23
22
21
20
19
18
17

STYLE 1
DEER-MOOSE

STYLE 2
DEER-MOOSE

STYLE 3
DEER-MOOSE

STYLE
2

STYLE
3

BLACK
EYES

Style 1.

BIRD EYES.

FISH EYE

ALLIGATOR

BEAR

DOG - FOX

CAT

WILD CAT

Cornered eyes are measured across

Styles and Sizes of Eyes

CHAP. XI

Sizes and Colors of Eyes---Wire

Glass eyes are used to replace the natural ones in all mounted work. You can get eyes of any dealer in naturalists supplies. We can recommend the goods sold by those mentioned in the last few pages in this book.

The eyes of different specimens vary very greatly in size, color and shapes of the pupil. All birds have a round black pupil and a uniformly colored iris; animals may have a round, elongated or vertical pupil and usually have the iris veined; fish have an irregular shaped pupil and the iris gold or silver with darker streaks.

For convenience, dealers list eyes under three styles: Style 1 has the pupil round and the iris any plain color or even clear glass. These are used for all birds. Style 2 may have a round or elongated pupil and has the iris veined. Style 3 is the same as Style 2 but has white corners. Either 2 or 3 are used for animals.

bird eye.

dog - fox

deer

cat

fish

black eye

Of course you should note the color of a specimen's eye before you skin it and get one to correspond; we give the following list of eyes suitable for a great many specimens. It will prove of assistance if you are mounting from skins and do not know what eyes the bird should have. The diagram gives the sizes and shapes of the different styles. Your dealer will send you a price list. All black eyes are much cheaper and are often used for small birds and squirrels where the natural eyes are dark brown.

NO.

1. *Brown*—Hummingbird; Bats.

2. *Brown (or black)*—Small Sparrows; Warblers; Chickadees; Mice.

3. *Brown (or black)*—Large Sparrows; Vireos.

4 and 5. *Brown*—Orioles; Bluebirds; Swallows; Blackbirds; smallest Sandpipers, Weasel.

6 and 7. *Brown*—Robins; Jays; Meadowlark; Shrikes; most Woodpeckers; Chipmunk. *Red*—Red-bellied Woodpecker; Anhinga. *Yellow*—Least Bittern, Rusty Grackle.

8 or 9. *Brown*—Crow; Partridge (Quail); Mallard; Scaup; Teal; Widgeon; Sparrow Hawk; Pigeon Hawk; Mink; Red Squirrel; Skunk; Rats. *Yellow*—Sharp-shinned Hawk; Pileated and Ivory

billed Woodpecker; Hooded Merganser; Redhead
(orange); Golden-eye; Snowy, Green, and Little
Blue Herons; Bufflehead. *Red*—Glossy Ibis; Can-
vas-back; Red-breasted and American Mergansers;
Louisiana Heron. *Green.*—Cormorants. *White*—
White Ibis.

10 or 11. *Brown (or hazel)*—Broad-wing
Hawk; Grouse, Woodcock; Gray and Fox Squirrels. *Yellow*—Hawk, Acadian, Long and Short-
eared Owls; Cooper Hawk; Bittern. *Blue-White*
—Flamingo.

12 or 13. *Brown*—Geese; Red-shouldered and
adult Red-tail Hawks; Duck and Rough-leg
Hawks; Raccoon. *Yellow*—Young Red-tail Hawk;
Herring and Black-backed Gulls. *Red*—Wood
Duck; Wood Ibis; Goshawk.

14 or 15. *Brown*—Golden and young Bald
Eagles; Rabbits and Hares. *Yellow*—Adult Bald
Eagle; Screech and Great Gray Owls; Fish Hawk;
young Night Heron. *Red*—Adult Night Herons;
Loons. *White*—White or Brown Pelicans.

16 or 17. *Brown*—Foxes and small Dogs;
Bear. *Black* (or blue-black)—Barred Owl.

18 to 20. *Brown*—Dog, Wolf, Grizzly. *Yellow*—Horned and Snowy Owls; Lynx.

22. Small Deer; Panther.

24. Large Deer; Tiger (yellow).

25 to 27. Elk and Moose; Mountain Sheep (pale brownish white); Caribou.

Approximate Sizes of Wire to Use

For taxidermy work you should always use annealed wire. If you cannot secure anything but spring wire you can anneal it by heating red hot and allowing it to cool gradually. It will be most convenient to buy wire of your supply dealer, cut and straightened. If you buy it in coils, you can straighten any size up to number 12 as follows:

Coil wire is straightened by stretching

It may be sharpened with a file, or by cutting obliquely with the cutters.

Fasten one end firmly in a vice, or bend it about a hook or a nail driven in the floor; reel off a piece about ten feet long, cut it and grasp the end firmly in the pliers. Pull and as soon as it stretches a bit it will remain straight. It should then be cut into 18 in. lengths as this is the most convenient length to handle. The following list will give you an idea of what sizes you will need. The sizes as given are for the leg wires of birds; except in the case of long-necked birds the neck wire can be one or two numbers smaller in size than the leg wires.

No. 26. This fine wire will come upon a spool; it is used for Hummingbirds, small Warblers and Titmice.

No. 24. You can get this either on a spool or in coil; use it for Warblers, Sparrows, Vireos and birds of like size.

No. 22. Suitable for Finches, Thrushes, Bluebirds, and Flycatchers.

No. 20. Small Sandpipers, Kingbirds, Grosbeaks, Orioles.

No. 18. Terns, large Sandpipers and Plover, Quail, Jays, Flickers, Robins, Grackles, Thrashers, Rats and Chipmunks.

No. 16. Yellowlegs, Black-bellied Plover, Doves, small Owls, Kingfishers, Mink, Red Squirrel.

California Partridge.

No. 14. Long, Short-eared and Barn Owls, Grebes, small Gulls, Coots, Hooded Merganser, Teal, Bufflehead, Ruddy Duck, Grouse, small Hawks, Crow, Gray Squirrel.

BobWhite.

No. 12. Large Owls, Hawks, Ducks, Gulls, Night Heron, Bittern, Skunk, Muskrat, Opossum, Woodchuck.

No. 10. Loon, Goose, Blue Heron, Spoonbill, Osprey, Wood Ibis, Raccoon.

No. 8. Flamingo, Pelicans, Eagles, Wild Cat, Fox.

American Elk

(Large mammals are mounted over a papier-mache covered manikin)

No. 6.   Swan, Sandhill and Whooping Cranes, Wild Turkeys.

1-4 in. rod for large Dogs, Wolves, Fawns.

1-2 in. rod for Deer, Caribou, Ostrich.

5-8 in. rod for Elk and Moose.

If you are in doubt at any time as to what size wire to use for a specimen, use the largest size; do not have your finished specimen "wabbly."

Large birds with spread wings should have a size larger wire than the same bird folded; the wings can have a size smaller wire than the legs. The tail wires should always be a couple of sizes smaller than the leg wires.

Barn Swallow.

Cliff Swallow.

CHAP. XII

Stands, Stumps, Rock, Foliage
Etc.

Stands for specimens intended as ornamental or decorative can be made as fancy as you wish. If you are making a scientific collection, either have all the specimens on severely plain mounts or, if you have plenty of room, try to make your case work so near natural as to defy detection.

A large collection of birds looks very well mounted on plain T perches for the perching birds, and flat boards for all others; the stands being all uniform leave nothing to attract the attention from the specimens, which of course are the main objects of a collection.

Our preference for a scientific collection is to have each group (male, female and young) on one stand, either a stump or suitable twig rising from a round, white base with no foliage. On following page is a group taken from our collection of Worcester County Birds. If you have an abundance

of room it is well to incorporate the nest and eggs
and natural surroundings for each group.

The same is true of a collection of mammals;
either mount them severely plain or take the space
to properly represent the group of each species
with its surroundings.

T Perches.—These are the simplest forms of
stands. You can easily make them out of round
doweling and pine stock of thickness to correspond
to the size. The method of construction can be
plainly seen on the marginal sketches opposite
this. These can be left in a rough state for temporary perches or can be finished a dead white color
for museum purposes.

Turned T Perches.—These are turned, usually
out of hard wood, on a lathe and finished with shellac and oil at the same time. These make excellent
stands for hawks and owls, and are often used on
birds for house decoration rather than the natural
stumps. The sketch opposite this shows a good
form for a turned stand.

Flat Stands.—Can be made of hard wood and
polished or of soft wood either painted or stained.
The edges should be beveled.

Black-poll Warbler
(An excellent method of mounting for museum exhibition)

Artificial Stumps, Rocks and Groundwork.—
This work is a good test for your skill and patience.
You can make your work crude or a very good
imitation of Nature, according to the degree of
perfection you have attained or the time you care
to put into it. Stumps, rocks and groundwork are
made in the same way, the only difference being in
the shapes and the final finish.

Make the bottom board of soft wood of a proper
size to accommodate the specimen for which it is intended, and bevel the edges. If the feet of your
specimen are to be upon the top of the rock or
stump you must make an upright and crosspiece of
wood in the proper place. The marginal sketches
opposite illustrate the method of making a stand
suitable for an eagle, heron or duck. It has one
crosspiece in the middle, this being intended for the
reception of the wires in the specimen's legs. Any
other prominent elevations may have a block of
wood to support the wire mosquito netting that is to
be tacked over the frame and along the edges of
the base. This frame can be dented to make a
rock of any shape or to make an uneven ground.
If you are making a stump, of course the wire
will be bent around your upright piece in a cir-
cular shape.

Artificial stump

Mix a batch of papier-mache (see Chapter 10) and squeeze it into the wire mesh leaving the outside rough or smooth as your subject may call for. A stump should have a few knots and broken branches fashioned on it with the papier-mache and the whole exterior should be grooved to represent the bark, this being done with a piece of wire or wood. Rockwork may have fine granite or mica sand sprinkled over it and lightly pushed into the papier-mache or it may be painted to imitate rocks after it is dry. A stump may be painted when dry or it may have mosses and litchens glued to it.

Wire frame for tree.

Artificial Trees and Branches.—We prefer to use natural branches when they can be obtained of the right shape for our needs, but it is often necessary to build artificial ones, especially for decorative purposes. A tree may be made for a single bird, or as we have often done, it may be made to fill a case six feet in height and to accommodate several hundred birds.

Wound with cloth strips

We will describe the making of a small branch suitable for a single Bluejay. The sketches opposite illustrate the method of making. Bore two awl holes, 3-4 in. apart, in the middle of your

beveled base board; take an 18 in. piece of No. 16
wire and bend it back so one arm will be about 5 in.
and the other 13; insert this through the holes in
the base from the bottom and twist the wires together above the base for about 3 in., and bend as
in Fig. A, twisting a shorter piece of wire on to
make the other two branches. Fig. 2 shows the
method of winding the tree with strips of cloth and
the way to fasten the artificial leaves upon it; the
last turn of the cloth about the end of the limb
should enclose the wire stem of the leaf and the
cloth be firmly tied to the wire with thread. The
trunk of the tree may have to have several strips
wound on to make it of a proper size; on large
trees, the trunk is usually wound with tow, before
using the cloth. At this stage the tree may be
painted with glue and covered with ground litchens,
or, and this is the better way, you can cover the
trunk and larger limbs with papier-mache and
when dry, color this to resemble the tree it is intended for. Entire collections should never be
placed upon these artificial trees as they are suitable only for commercial or decorative purposes.

Fastening leaves on.

Stand finished.

Artificial Leaves and Ferns.—You can buy these
already made of your dealer in naturalists' supplies. They come put up in gross lots. If you have

Deer Head

(Mounted very obliquely on a rustic panel)

a couple of varieties of small ferns and some small
oak, maple and elm leaves, and perhaps a few
aquatic leaves it will answer most requirements that
you will have for artificial foliage. Leaves, ferns
and grasses can be made out of heavy, starched
cloth such as is used for window curtains; cut
pieces the exact shape and size you wish the leaves;
glue a piece of No. 26 wire the whole length on the
back of the leaf and let it extend beyond to form a
stem; wax the leaf and the wire on the back of it;
by laying the leaf on a soft board you can make
the proper creases and veins with a wire or stick;
you must now paint the leaf its natural color; after
having been fastened to the branch the wire must
also be waxed and painted.

Natural Leaves.—Some kinds of leaves can be
preserved for case decoration by drying them in a
box of sand and painting them their natural colors.
These will be very fragile and should not be used
except under glass. Dried grasses and rushes, when
properly colored make excellent case decorations.

Moss.—Lichens and tree mosses of all kinds dry
well and can be used either dead color or dyed pale
green. Your supply dealer will probably have
French moss and dyed lace moss for sale.

For case decoration it is well to always have on

hand a supply of dead leaves, chestnut-burs, twigs, etc.

Winter Scenes.—After a stump, rock or piece of groundwork is made, as previously described, it can readily be made into a snow scene as follows:— Dissolve 1 ounce of pulverized glue in 1 pint of boiling water and add 4 ounces of whiting. As soon as this is cool it is ready for use; wherever you want snow on the base, paint it with this whiting and glue mixture and then sprinkle on a few flakes of Mica Flakes. The foliage and grasses may also have touches of this snow and you will have a very frosty stand; icicles, made as described in Chapter 10, can be attached to rockwood or stumps.

CHAP. XIII
Prices for Mounting Specimens

There are no fixed prices for taxidermy work but those of expert taxidermists for the best of work will average about the same all over the country. The following schedule of prices is averaged from ours and other leading taxidermists.

We have frequently seen specimens mounted for half these prices or less, but even that was more than they were worth. If you are going to do taxidermy, make up your mind to become an expert, do the best work and get paid accordingly.

Birds

$1.25.—Hummers, Warblers, Sparrows and other birds up to the size of a Bluebird. The same birds with spread wings—$1.50.

$1.50.—Jays, Robins, Flickers, Blackbirds, Meadowlark and others of same size. Spread—$1.75.

$1.75.—Kingfisher, Sharp-shinned, Sparrow and Pigeon Hawks, Acadian Owl, large Plover, Bob White, Woodcock, Petrel, Common Terns, etc. Spread, $2.00.

Moose

(A plain, oval, oak shield makes an excellent mounting for any
head, and especially for large ones)

$2.00.—Grebe, Guillemot, Coot, Doves and Pigeons, Screech and Hawk Owls, Paraquets, Pileated Woodpeckers, etc. Spread, $2.25.

$2.50.—Puffin, Murre, Laughing and Bonaparte Gull, Green and Little Blue Heron, Spruce Grouse, Cooper and Broad-wing Hawks, etc. Wings spread, $2.75.

$3.00.—Kittiwake and Ring-bill Gulls, Green and Blue-wing Teals, Snow and Louisiana Herons, Ptarmigan, Grouse, Red-shouldered Hawk, Long and Short-eared Owls, etc. Wings spread, $3.50.

$3.50.—Jaegers, Calif. Gull, Heermann Gull, Caspian Tern, Shearwaters, Anhinga, Shoveller, Ring-neck and Old Squaw Ducks, White and Glossy Ibises, Bittern, Night Heron, Prairie Hen and Sharp-tail Grouse, Marsh, Gos, and Red-tail Hawks, Barn and Barred Owls. Wings spread, $4.00.

$4.00.—Herring Gull, Crested Cormorants, Mallard, Redhead, Canvasback and Scoter Ducks. Spread, $4.50.

$5.00.—Loons, Black-backed Gull, Booby Cormorant, Tropic Birds, Eider Duck, Brant, Spoonbills, etc. Wings spread, $5.50.

$6.00.—Gannet, Brown Pelican, Man-of-war Bird, Geese, Blue Heron, etc. Spread, $6.50.

$10.00.—White Pelican, Eagles, Flamingo.
Spread, $12.00.

$12.00.—Swan.

Animals

$1.50.—Mice, Moles, etc.

$2.00.—Rats, Chipmunk, Red Squirrel, Weasel.

$2.50.—Gray Squirrels.

$4.00.—Woodchuck, Muskrat, Opossum.

$8.00 to $12.00.—Coons, Foxes, Wild Cat.

$15.00 to $25.00.—Dogs, Coyotes and Wolves.

$25.00 to $75.00.—Leopards, Sheep, Goats and Deer.

Heads

Deer, $10.00 to $15.00; Moose, $25.00 to $35.00; Caribou, $15.00 to $25.00; Elk, $25.00; Sheep and Goats, $15.00 to $25.00.

Miscellaneous

Fish, from $5.00 up, reckoning about a dollar a pound up to fifteen pounds. Reptiles, from $5.00 up.

CHAP. XIV

List of Birds of North America, together with a fair valuation of the eggs, skins and mounted specimens of each.

This list is carefully prepared so that our readers may have a basis for exchange with collectors in other parts of the country. The values as given are for first class specimens; of course other than first class ones have very little value anyway.

The numbers before each name are those given to the different species by the American Ornithologists' Union and should be used in marking eggs. Where these numbers are in brackets, it signifies that the bird can hardly be called American, and it has occurred but once or twice and probably by accident.

A star following the price of the egg means that the price is for European collected specimens. In such cases American eggs of the same species would be higher.

	Eggs	Skins	Mounted
1 Æchmophorus occidentalis Western Grebe ....$	.25	$ 2.00	$ 4.50
2 Colymbus holbœllii Holbœll's Grebe	.50	2.50	5.00
3 Colymbus auritus Horned Grebe	.20	1.50	4.00
4 Colymbus nigricollis californicus American Eared Grebe	.15	1.50	3.50
5 Colymbus dominicus brachybterus St. Domingo Grebe	.35	1.00	3.50

6 Podilymbus podiceps
Pied-billed Grebe ....$ .10 $ 1.00 $ 3.50
7 Gavia imber
Loon 1.50   4.00   8.00
8 Gavia adamsii
Yellow-billed Loon 8.00   10.00   15.00
9 Gavia arctica
Black-throated Loon 1.50   7.00   12.00
10 Gavia pacifica
Pacific Loon 2.00   6.00   10.00
11 Gavia lumme
Red-throated Loon .... .75*   3.00   6.00
12 Lunda cirrhata
Tufted Puffin .... .50   2.50   5.50
13 Fratercula arctica
Puffin .... .20   2.00   5.00
13aFratercula arctica naumanni
Large-billed Puffin 1.00   6.00   9.00
14 Fratercula corniculata
Horned Puffn 2.00   4.50   8.00
15 Cerorhinca monocerata
Rhinoceros Auklet 3.00   6.00   9.00
16 Ptychoramphus aleuticus
Cassin's Auklet 1.50   5.00   8.00
17 Cyclorrhynchus psittaculus
Paroquet Auklet 3.00   5.00   8.00
18 Simorhynchus cristatellus
Crested Auklet 3.00   4.50   7.00
19 Simorhynchus pygmæus
Whiskered Auklet 2.50   4.50   7.50

20 Simorhynchus pusillus
 Least Auklet 2.50 4.50 7.00
21 Synthliboramphus antiquus
 Ancient Murrelet 3.00 5.00 8.00
23 Brachyramphus marmoratus
 Marbled Murrelet 4.00 4.00 7.00
24 Brachyramphus kittlitzii
 Kittlitz's Murrelet 5.00 5.00 8.00
25 Brachyramphus hypoleucus
 Xantus's Murrelet 5.00 5.00 8.00
26 Brachyramphus craveri
 Craveri's Murrelet 4.00 5.00 8.00
27 Cepphus grylle
 Black Guillemot .... .25 2.00 5.25
28 Cepphus mandtii
 Mandt's Guillemot .... .75 3.50 6.75
29 Cepphus columba
 Pigeon Guillemot .... .50 2.00 4.50
30 Uria troile
 Murre .... .20 2.00 5.00
30a Uria troile californica
 California Murre .... .20 2.00 5.00
31 Uria lomvia
 Brunnich's Murre .... .25 2.00 5.00
31a Uria lomvia arra
 Pallas's Murre .... .50 3.00 6.00
32 Alca torda
 Razor-billed Auk .... .25 2.00 5.00
33 Plautus impennis
 Great Auk .... 1.00 (cast)

34 Alle alle
    Dovekie ....$ 1.25 $ 1.50 $ 3.25
35 Megalestris skua
    Skua 50*   3.00   6.50
36 Stercorarius pomarinus
    Pomarine Jæger 2.50*   3.50   6.00
37 Stercorarius parasiticus
    Parasitic Jæger 50*   2.00   5.00
38 Stercorarius longicaudus
    Long-tailed Jæger 1.50*   3.50   6.00
39 Paqophila alba
    Ivory Gull 5.00*   4.50   7.50
40 Rissa tridactyla
    Kittiwake 40*   1.50   4.50
40a Rissa tridactyla pollicaris
    Pacific Kittiwake 1.50   2.50   5.50
41 Rissa brevirostris
    Red-legged Kittiwake 2.50   6.50 10.00
42 Larus glaucus
    Glaucous Gull 75*   4.00   7.00
42.1 Larus barrovianus
    Point Barrow Gull 3.50   5.00   8.00
43 Larus Leucopterus
    Iceland Gull 1.25*   4.00   8.00
44 Larus glaucescens
    Glaucous-winged Gull 2.00   3.00   6.50
45 Larus kumlieni
    Kumlien's Gull 3.50   5.00   8.00
46 Larus nelsoni
    Nelson's Gull 5.00   8.00

47 Larus marinus
      Great Black-backed Gull ....$ .50 $ 3.00 $ 7.00

48 Larus schistisagus
      Slaty-backed Gull 5.00   8.00

49 Larus occidentalis
      Western Gull 20   3.00   6.00

[50] Larus affinis
       Siberian Gull 8.00   12.00

51 Larus argentatus
      Herrin Gull 20   2.00   4.00

52 Larus vegæ
      Vega Gull 2.00   2.00   5.00

53 Larus californicus
      California Gull 20   2.00   5.00

54 Larus delawarensis
      Ring-billed Gull 20   1.00   3.50

55 Larus brachyrhynchus
      Short-billed Gull 1.50   3.00   5.00

[56] Larus canus
       Mew Gull 20   1.75   4.00

57 Larus heermanni
      Heermann's Gull 5.00   5.00   8.00

58 Larus atricilla
      Laughing Gull 20   1.50   3.50

59 Larus franklinii
      Franklin's Gull 35   1.50   3.50

60 Larus philadelphia
      Bonaparte's Gull 2.00   1.50   4.00

[60.1] Larus minutus
         Little Gull 2.50   4.50

61 Rhodostethia rosea
    Ross's Gull .... $ 4.00 $ 6.50
62 Xema sabinii
    Gull-billed Tern ....$ .20   1.00   3.00
63 Gelochelidon nilotica
    Sabine's Gull 3.00   5.00   8.00
64 Sterna caspia
    Caspian Tern 50   2.00   4.50
65 Sterna maxima
    Royal Tern 40   3.00   5.00
66 Sterna elegans
    Elegant Tern ....".........   5.00   8.00   10.00
67 Sterna sandvicensis acu flavida
    Cabot's Tern 40   1.50   4.00
[68]Sterna trudeaui
    Trudeau's Tern 5.00   8.00
69 Sterna forsteri
    Forster's Tern 10   1.00   3.00
70 Sterna hirundo
    Common Tern 10   1.00   3.00
71 Sterna paradisæa
    Arctic Tern 10   1.00   3.00
72 Sterna dougalli
    Roseate Tern 15   1.25   3.50
73 Sterna aleutica
    Aleutian Tern 2.00   3.00   5.00
74 Sterna antillarum
    Least Tern 20   1.00   3.00
75 Sterna fuliginosa
    Sooty Tern 25   2.50   4.50

[76] Sterna anæthetus
 Bridled Tern ....$ 1.00 $ 3.00 $ 5.50
77 Hydrochelidon nigra surinamensis
 Black Tern .... .10 1.00 3.00
[78] Hydrochelidon leucoptera
 White-winged Black Tern .... .50* 2.00 4.00
79 Anous Stolidus
 Noddy .... .50 3.00 5.00
80 Rynchops nigra
 Black Skimmer .... .15 1.00 3.00
81 Diomedea nigripes
 Black-footed Albatross 5.00 10.00 18.00
82 Diomedea albatrus
 Short-tailed Albatross 5.00 10.00 18.00
[83] Thalassogeron culminatus
 Yellow-nosed Albatross 3.00 10.00 20.00
84 Phœbetria fuliginosa
 Sooty Albatross 3.00 10.00 18.00
[85] Ossifraga gigantea
 Giant Fulmar 5.00 10.00 15.00
86 Fulmarus glacialis
 Fulmar .... .75* 4.50 8.00
86a Fulmarus glacialis minor
 Lesser Fulmar 4.00 8.00
86b Fulmarus glacialis glupischa
 Pacific Fulmar 2.00 5.00 9.00
86c Fulmarus glacialis rodgersii
 Rodger's Fulmar 2.50 6.00 12.00
87 Fulmarus glacialoides
 Slender-billed Fulmar 10.00 14.00

88 Puffinus borealis
    Cory's Shearwater .... $ 5.00 $ 8.00
89 Puffnus major
    Greater Shearwater ....$ 3.00   2.50   6.00
90 Puffinus puffinus
    Manx Shearwater 1.00   3.00   5.50
91 Puffinus creatopus
    Pink-footed Shearwater ....
92 Puffinus auduboni
    Audubon's Shearwater 1.00   4.00   7.00
93 Puffinus opisthornelas
    Black-vented Shearwater 2.50   4.00   7.00
94 Puffinus fuliqinosus
    Sooty Shearwater 3.00   4.00   7.00
95 Puffinus griseus
    Dark-bodied Shearwater ....
96 Puffinus tenuirostris
    Slender-billed Shearwater ....
[97]Puffinus cinereus
    Black-tailed Shearwater ....
[98]Æstrelata hasitata
    Black-caped Petrel ....
[99]Æstrelata scalaris
    Scaled Petrel ....
100 Æstrelata fisheri
    Fisher's Petrel ....
[101]Bulweria bulweri
    Bulwer's Petrel ....
[102]Daption capensis
    Pintado Petrel 5.00   8.00

103	Halocyptena microsoma		
	Least Petrel	$ 5.00	$ 8.00
104	Procellaria pelagica		
	Stormy Petrel ....$ .50	3.00	5.00
105	Oceanodroma furcata		
	Fork-tailed Petrel 2.00	4.00	7.00
106	Oceanodroma leucorhoa		
	Leach's Petrel 20	1.25	3.00
106.1	Oceanodroma macrodactyla		
	Gaudalupe Petrel		
107	Oceanodroma melania		
	Black Petrel		
108	Oceanodroma homochroa		
	Ashy Petrel 3.00	5.00	8.00
109	Oceanites oceanicus		
	Wilson's Petrel	1.50	3.50
[110]	Fregetta grallaria		
	White-bellied Petrel 2.00	3.00	6.00
111	Pelagodroma marina		
	White-faced Petrel 1.50	6.00	9.00
112	Phæthon flavirostris		
	Yellow-billed Tropic Bird 2.50	5.00	10.00
113	Phæthon æthereus		
	Red-billed Tropic Bird 3.00	5.00	10.00
[114]	Sula cyanops		
	Blue faced Booby 2.00	5.00	10.00
114.1	Sula nebouxii		
	Blue footed Booby 5.00	7.00	12.00
115	Sula sula		
	Booby 1.75	5.00	10.00

115.1 Sula brewsteri
Brewster's Booby ....
[116] Sula piscator
Red-footed Booby .... $ 6.00 $12.00
117 Sula bassana
Ganet ....$ .35   4.00   8.00
118 Anhinga anhinga
Anhinga 25   3.50   7.00
119 Phalacrocorax carbo
Cormorant 25   3.50   6.50
120 Phalacrocorax dilophus
Double-crested Cormorant 25   3.00   6.00
120a Phalacrocorax dilophus floridanus
Florida Cormorant 25   2.50   5.50
120b Phalacrocorax dilphus cincinatus
White-crested Cormorant 25   3.00   6.00
120c Phalacrocorax dilphus albociliatus
Farallone Cormorant 25   3.00   6.00
121 Phalacrocorax mexicanus
Mexican Cormorant 1.00   3.00   6.00
122 Phalacrocorax penicillatus
Brandt's Cormorant 25   3.50   6.00
123 Phalacrocorax pelagicus
Pelagic Cormorant 1.00   5.00   9.00
123a Phalacrocorax pelagicus robustus
Violet-green Cormorant 1.00   4.00   7.00
123b Phalacrocorax pelagicas resplendens
Baird's Cormorant 25   3.50   7.00
124 Phalacrocorax urile
Red-faced Cormorant 1.00   5.00   8.00

125 Pelecanus erythrorhnchos
   American White Pelican ....$ .25 $ 7.00 $15.00
126 Pelecanus fucsus
   Brown Pelican .... .20   6.00   12.00
127 Pelecanus californicus
   California Brown Pelican .... .20   6.00   12.00
128 Fregata aquilla
   Man-'o-War Bird 1.00   6.00   12.00
129 Merganser americanus
   American merganser 1.50   1.75   5.00
130 Merganser serrator
   Red-breasted Merganser .... .25   1.50   4.50
131 Lophodytes cucullatus
   Hooded Merganser 1.50   2.00   5.00
132 Anas boschas
   Mallard .... .20   1.75   5.00
133 Anas obscura
   Black Duck .... .40   1.75   5.00
134 Anas fulvigula
   Florida Duck 1.00   2.50   5.00
134aAnas fulvigula maculosa
   Mottled Duck 1.00   3.00   6.00
135 Chaulelasmus strepera
   Gadwall .... .50   2.00   5.00
136 Mareca penelope
   Widgeon .... .25* 2.00   5.00
[137]Mareca americana
   Baldpate .... .75   2.00   5.00
[138]Nettion carolinesis
   European Teal .... .20* 2.00   4.50

139 Nettion carolinensis
    Green-winged Teal ....$ .20 $ 1.25 $ 4.00
140 Querquedula discors
    Blue-winged Teal .... .20   1.25   4.00
141 Querquedula cyanoptera
    Cinnamon Teal .... .20   2.00   5.00
142 Spatula clypeata
    Shoveller .... .30   2.00   4.00
143 Dafila acuta
    Pintail .. .. .20* 2.00   5.00
144 Aix sponsa
    Wood Duck .... .75   2.50   5.00
[145]Netta rufina
    Rufous-crested Duck 2.00   2.75   5.00
146 Aythya americana
    Redhead .... .35   2.50   5.00
147 Aythya vallisneria
    Canvas-back 1.25   2.00   5.00
148 Aythya marila nearctica
    American Scaup Duck .... .60* 2.00   5.00
149 Aythya affinis
    Lesser Scaup Duck................ .75* 2.00   5.00
150 Aythya collaris
    Ring-necked Duck 1.25   1.75   5.00
151 Clangula clangula americana
    American Golden-eye 1.25   1.75   5.00
152 Clangula islandica
    Barrow's Golden-eye 1.00   2.25   5.50
153 Chariotonetta albeola
    Buffle-head 2.00   1.50   4.00

154 Hanelda hyemalis
    Old-squaw ....$ .40 $ 2.00 $ 5.00
155 Histrionicus histrionicus
    Harlequin Duck 1.00* 3.00   6.00
156 Camptolaimus labradorius
    Labrador Duck ....
157 Eniconetta stelleri
    Steller's Duck 5.00   6.00 10.00
158 Arctonetta fischeri
    Spectacled Elder 2.50 12.00 18.00
159 Somateria mollissima borealis
    Northern Eider .... .50   3.50   7.00
160 Somateria dresseri
    American Eider .... .20   3.00   7.00
161 Somateria v-nigra
    Pacific Eider 1.00   4.00   8.00
162 Somateria spectabilis
    King Eider 1.50   8.00 12.00
163 Oidemia americana
    American Scoter 2.00   2.25   5.00
[164]Oidemia fusca
    Velvet Scoter .... .50* 2.50   6.00
165 Oidemia deglandi
    White-winged Scoter 2.50   2.50   5.50
166 Oidemia perspicillata
    Surf Scoter 2.50   2.25   5.50
167 Erismatura rubida
    Ruddy Duck .... .35   1.50   4.50
[168]Nomonyx dominiscus
    Masked Duck . ...

169 Chen hyperborea Lesser Snow Goose ....$		$ 4.00	$ 8.00
169aChen hyperborean nivalis Greater Snow Goose..............		4.00	8.00
169.1 Chen cærulescens Blue Goose		4.00	8.00
170 Chen rossii Ross's Snow Goose		6.00	10.00
[171]Anser albifrons White-fronted Goose	1.00*	3.50	8.00
171aAnser albifrons gambeli Am. White-fronted Goose	1.00*	3.50	8.00
172 Branta canadensis Canada Goose	1.00	3.50	7.00
172aBranta canadensis hutchingii Hutchin's Goose	1.50	3.50	8.00
172bBranta canadensis occidentalis White-cheeked Goose	2.50	4.50	9.00
172cBranta canadensis minima Cackling Goose	4.00	6.00	10.00
173 Branta bernicla Brant	3.50	3.00	6.50
174 Branta nigricans Black Brant	3.50	4.00	6.50
[175]Branta leucopsis Barnacle Goose		3.50	7.00
176 Philacte canagica Emperor Goose	4.00	15.00	20.00
177 Dendrocygna autumnalis Black-bellied Tree Duck	2.00	1.75	5.00

178 Dendrocygna fulva
   Fulvous Tree-duck ....$ 2.00 $ 1.75 $ 5.00
[179]Olor cygnus
   Whooping Swan 1.50* 10.00 20.00
180 Olor columbianus
   Whistling Swan 2.50 7.00 16.50
181 Olor buccinator
   Trumpeter Swan 4.00 8.00 20.00
182 Phœnicopterus ruber
   American Flamingo 1.00 15.00 25.00
183 Ajaja ajaja
   Roseate Spoonbill 1.00 7.00 10.00
184 Guara alba
   White Ibis .... .35 2.00 6.00
[185]Gura rubra
   Scarlet Ibis 3.00 10.00 15.00
186 Plegadis autumnalis
   Glossy Ibis .... .35 3.50 7.00
187 Plegadis guarauna
   White-faced Glossy Ibis .... .35 3.50 6.50
188 Tantalus loculator
   Wood Ibis .... .35 4.00 9.00
[189]Mycteria americana
   Jabiru 7.50 10.00 15.00
190 Botaurus lentiginosus
   American Bittern .... .75 1.50 4.50
191 Ardetta exilis
   Least Bittern .... .20 1.25 3.50
191.1 Ardetta neoxena
   Cory's Least Bittern 1.50 2.50 4.50

192 Ardea occidentalis
     Great White Heron. . . . .$ 1.00 $15.00 $20.00

194 Ardea herodias
     Great Blue Heron 25 3.00 8.00

194b Ardea wardi
     Ward's Heron 40 5.00 10.00

[195] Ardea cinerea
     European Blue Heron 25 2.50 8.00

196 Herodias egretta
     American Egret 30 3.50 7.00

197 Egretta candidissima
     Snowy Heron 20 3.50 7.00

198 Dichromanassa rufescens
     Reddish Egret 20 2.25 6.00

199 Hydranassa tricolor ruficollis
     Louisiana Heron 10 1.25 4.50

200 Florida coerulea
     Little Blue Heron 10 1.25 4.50

201 Butorides virescens
     Green Heron . . . . .10 .75 3.00

201a Butorides virescens frazari
     Frazar's Green Heron . . . .

202 Nycticorax nycticorax nævins
     Black-crowned Night Heron 10 1.50 4.50

203 Nycticorax violasceous
     Yellow-crowned Night Heron. 20 2.50 5.00

204 Grus americana
     Whooping Crane 3.00 18.00 25.00

205 Grus canadensis
     Little Brown Crane 5.00 6.00 10.00

206 Grus mexicana			
Sandhill Crane	$ 3.00	$ 6.00	$10.00
207 Aramus giganteus			
Limpkin	.75	3.50	6.00
208 Rallus elegans			
King Rail	.20	1.50	3.50
209 Rallus beldingi			
Belding's Rail			
210 Rallus obsoletus			
California Clapper Rail	.35	2.00	4.00
211 Rallus crepitans			
Clapper Rail	.10	1.00	3.00
211aRallus crepitans saturatus			
Louisiana Clapper Rail	.35	1.50	3.50
211cRallus longirostris caribæus			
Carribean Clapper Rail	.75	3.00	5.00
211.1 Rallus scottii			
Scott's Rail		1.50	3.00
212 Rallus virginianus			
Virginia Rail	.20	.60	2.50
[213]Porzana porzana			
Spotted Crake	.30*	1.60	3.50
214 Porzana carolina			
Sora	.10	.40	2.00
215 Porzana noveboracensis			
Yellow Rail	3.00	3.50	5.00
216 Porzana jamaicensis			
Black Rail	3.00	3.00	5.00
216aPorzana jamaicensis coturniculus			
Farallone Rail	3.00	5.00	7.00

[217]Crex crex			
Corn Crake ....$	.20 $	1.25 $	3.50
218 Ionoris martinica			
Purple Gallinule	.25	1.50	3.50
219 Gallinula galeata			
Florida Gallinule	.10	.75	2.75
[220]Fulica atra			
European Coot	.15*	1.25	3.50
221 Fulica americana			
American Coot	.10	1.00	3.50
222 Crymaphilus fulicarius			
Red Phalarope	1.50	3.50	5.00
223 Phalaropus lobatus			
Northern Phalarope	.75	1.50	3.00
224 Phalaropus tricolar			
Wilson's Phalarope	.75	.75	2.50
225 Recurvirostra americana			
American Avocet	.50	1.25	3.50
226 Himantopus mexicanus			
Black-necked Stilt	.50	1.50	3.50
[227]Scolopax rusticola			
European Woodcock	1.75*	1.50	3.50
228 Philohela minor			
American Woodcock	1.00	1.50	3.50
[229]Gallinago gallinago			
European Snipe	.35*	1.25	2.75
230 Gallinago delicata			
Wilson's Snipe	1.50	.75	2.25
231 Macrorhamphus griseus			
Dowitcher	2.50	1.00	3.00

232 Macrorhamphus scolopaceus
    Long-billed Dowitcher ....$ 2.50 $ 1.00 $ 3.00

233 Micropalama himantopus
    Stilt Sandpiper 3.00   1.25   3.00

234 Tringa canutus
    Knot 5.00   1.00   3.00

235 Arquatella maritima
    Purple Sandpiper .... 2.00   .60   2.00

236 Arquatella couesi
    Aleutian Sandpiper 3.00   2.50   4.00

237 Arquatella ptilocnemis
    Pribilof Sandpiper 3.00   2.50   4.00

238 Actodromas acuminata
    Sharp-tailed Sandpiper 6.00   3.50   5.00

239 Actodromas maculata
    Pectoral Sandpiper .... 2.00   .50   2.00

240 Actodromas fuscicollis
    White-rumped Sandpiper .... 3.00   .75   2.75

241 Actodromas bardii
    Baird's Sandpiper 2.00   1.00   2.75

242 Actodromas minutilla
    Least Sandpiper .... 2.00   .30   2.00

[242.1]Actodromas damancensis
    Long-toed Stint 5.00   2.00   4.00

[243]Pelida alpina
    Dunlin .... .35*   1.50   3.50

243aPelida alpina pacifica
    Red-backed Sandpiper .... 3.00   .75   2.50

244 Erotia ferruginea
    Curlew Sandpiper 5.00   1.50   3.50

[245]Eurynorhynchus pygmæus
　　Spoon-bill Sandpiper . . . .
246 Ereunetes pusillus
　　Semipaumated Sandpiper . . . .$ 3.00 ⚹ .10 ⚹ 2.50
247 Ereunetes occidentalis
　　Western Sandpiper . . . . 2.00　1.00　2.50
248 Calidris arenaria
　　Sanderling . . . .　　　.75　2.25
249 Limosa fedoa
　　Marbled Godwit . . . . 1.25　1.50　3.25
250 Limosa lapponica baueri
　　Pacific Godwit . . . . 3.00　4.50　7.00
251 Limosa hæmastica
　　Hudsonian Godwit . . . . 2.50　1.75　3.50
[252]Limosa limosa
　　Black-tailed Godwit .... 3.00　1.50　3.50
[253]Totanus nebularius
　　Green-shank . . . . 2.50*　2.00　4.50
254 Totanus melanolecus
　　Greater Yellow-legs .... 5.00　1.00　3.00
255 Totanus flavipes
　　Yellow-legs .... 2.50　.75　2.50
256 Heledromas salitarius
　　Solitary Sandpiper . . . . 4.00　.75　2.00
256aHeledromas solitarius cinnamomeus
　　West. Solitary Sandpiper.. . . . . . 5.00　1.00　3.00
257 Heledromas ochorpus
　　Green Sandpiper . . . . 2.00*　2.00　4.00
258 Symphemia semipalmata
　　Willet . . . . .40　1.50　4.50

258aSymphemia semipalmata inornata
    Western Willet ....$ .50 $ 1.50 $ 4.50
259 Heteractitis incanus
    Wandering Tatler 5.00   2.50   4.50
[260]Pavoncella pugnax
    Ruff .... .20*   1.50   4.00
261 Bartramia longicauda
    Bartramian Sandpiper .... .35   .75   2.75
262 Tryngites subruficollis
    Buff-breasted Sandpiper 3.00   1.00   2.75
263 Actitis macularia
    Spotted Sandpiper .... .15   .40   2.00
264 Numenius longirostris
    Long-billed Curlew 1.00   1.50   3.50
265 Numenius hudsonicus
    Hudsonian Curlew 3.00   1.50   3.50
266 Numenius borealis
    Eskimo Curlew 2.00   2.00   4.00
[267]Numenius phæopus
    Whimbrel .... .35*   1.50   4.50
[268]Numenius tahitiencis
    Bristle-thighed Curlew ....
[269]Vanelus vanellus
    Lapwing .... .15*   1.50   3.00
270 Squatarola squatarola
    Black-bellied Plover 4.00   2.00   4.00
[271]Charadrius apricarius
    Golden Plover .... .40*   2.00   4.00
272 Charadrius dominicus
    American Golden Plover 2.00   2.50   4.50

254   GUIDE TO TAXIDERMY

272aCharadrius dominicus fulvus
  Pacific Golden Plover..............$ 2.00 $ 3.00 $ 5.00
273 Oxyechus vociferus
  Kildeer 20   .50   2.00
274 Ægialitis semipalmata
  Semipalmated Plover .... 1.00   .40   2.50
275 Ægialitis hiaticula
  Ring Plover 20*   1.00   2.50
[276]Ægialitis dubia
  Little Ring Plover 20*   1.25   2.50
277 Ægialitis meloda
  Piping Plover 75   1.00   3.00
277aÆgialitis meloda circumcincta
  Belted Piping Sandpiper 75   1.00   3.00
278 Ægialitis nivosa
  Snowy Plover 50   1.00   3.50
[279]Ægialitis mongola
  Mongolian Plover 3.00   3.00   5.00
280 Ægialitis wilsonia
  Wilson's Plover 25   .50   2.50
281 Podasocys mountanius
  Mountain Plover 1.00   1.00   3.00
282 Aphriza virgata
  Surf Bird 2.50   5.00
283Arenarian interpres
  Turnstone 2.00   1.00   3.00
284 Arenaria melanocephala
  Black Turnstone 3.00   1.50   3.50
[285]Hæmatopus ostralegus
  Oyster-catcher 25*   1.50   4.00

286 Hæmatopus palliatus
   American Oyster-catcher ....$ .75 $ 1.50 $ 4.00
286.1Tæmatopus frazari
   Frazar's Oyster-catcher ....
287 Hæmatopus bachmani
   Black Oyster-catcher 1.75   3.00   5.50
[288]Jacana spinosa
   Mexican Jacana 2.50   1.50   3.50
289 Colinus virginianus
   Bob-white 10   1.00   2.50
289aColinus virginianus floridanus
   Florida Bob-white 10   1.00   2.75
289bColinus virginianus texanus
   Texan Bob-white 10   1.60   4.00
291 Colinus ridgwayi
   Masked Bob-white 10.00   13.00
292 Oreortyx pictus
   Mountain Partridge 1.00   1.50   3.50
292aOreortyx pictus plumiferus
   Plumer Partridge 75   1.50   3.75
292bOreortyx pictus confinus
   San Pedro Partridge 2.00   2.50   5.00
293 Callipepla squamata
   Scaled Partridge 75   1.00   2.75
293aCallipepla squamata castanogastris
   Chestnut-bellied Scaled Partridge.... .35   .75   2.50
294 Lophortyx californica
   California Partridge 10   1.00   2.75
294aLophortyx californica vallicola
   Valley Partridge 20   .75   2.50

295Lophortyx gambelii
Gambel's Partridge ....$ .25 $ 1.50 $ 3.00
296 Cyrtonyx montezumæ mearnsi
Mearns' Partridge .... .200   5.00   7.00
297 Dendrapus obscurus
Dusky Grouse 1.50   2.00   5.00
297aDendragapus obscurus fulginosus
Sooty Grouse .... .85   2.00   5.00
297mDendragapus obscurus richardsonii
Richardson's Grouse 1.50   4.00   6.50
298 Dendragapus canadensis
Canada Grouse 1.50   1.25   3.50
299 Dendragapus franklinii
Franklin's Grouse 3.50   2.50   5.00
300 Bonasa umbellus
Ruffed Grouse .... .30   1.25   4.00
300aBonasa umbellus togata
Canadian Ruffed Grouse .... .40   1.25   4.00
300bBonasa umbellus umbelloides
Gray Ruffed Grouse.............. .75   3.00   5.50
300cBonasa umbellus sabini
Oregon Ruffed Grouse .... .40   1.25   3.00
301 Lagopus lagopus
Willow Ptarmigan 1.00   1.25   3.00
301aLagopus lagopus alleni
Allen's Ptarmigan 3.00   5.00
302 Lagopus rupestris
Rock Ptarmigan .... .50*   3.00   5.00
302aLagopus rupestris reinhardii
Reinhard't Ptarmigan 2.50   3.00   5.00

302bLagopus rupestris nelsoni
  Nelson's Ptarmigan ....
302cLagopus rupestris atkhensis
  Turner's Ptarmigan ....
303 Lagopus welchi
  Welch's Ptarmigan ....
304 Lagopus leucurus
  White-tailed Ptarmigan ....$ 5.00 $ 3.00 $ 5.00
305 Tympanuchus americanus
  Prairie Hen .... .20   1.25   3.50
305aTympanuchus americanus attwateri
  Atwater's Prairie Hen .... .75   3.00   5.00
306 Tympanuchus cupido
  Heath Hen 100.00 100.00
307 Tympanuchus pallidictinctus
  Lesser Prairie Hen 1.50   2.25   5.00
308 Pediocætes phasianellus
  Sharp-tailed Grouse 2.50   1.25   4.00
308aPediocætes phasianellus columbianus
  Colu. Sharp-tailed Grouse........... .50   1.50   4.00
308bPediocætes phasianellus campestris
  Prairie Sharp-tailed Grouse .... .50   3.00   5.00
309 Centrocercus urophasianus
  Sage Grouse 50   3.00   7.00
310 Meleagris gallopavo
  Wild Turkey 75   8.00   16.00
310aMelagris gallopavo mexicana
  Mexican Turkey 1.00   8.00   16.00
310bMeleagris gallopavo osceola
  Florida Wild Turkey 2.00   12.00   20.00

310cMeleagros gallopavo intermedia
Rio Grande Turkey ....$ 2.00 $10.00 $18.00

311 Ortalis vetula maccalli
Chachalaca .... .75 1.00 3.50

312 Colnmba fasciata
Band-tailed Pigeon 1.00 1.50 3.50

312aColnmba·fasciata vioscæ
Viosca's Pigeon 3.00 3.00 5.00

313 Columba flavirostris
Bed-billed Pigeon 1.00 1.25 3.00

314 Colnmba leucocephala
White-crowned Pigeon 1.00 3.00 5.00

315 Ectopistes migratorius
Passenger Pigeon 2.00 5.00 8.00

316 Zenaidura macronra
Mourning Dove .... .05 .50 2.50

317 Zenaida zenaida
Zenaida Dove 1.00 3.50 5.50

318 Laptotila fulventris brachyptera
White-fronted Dove .... .35 1.25 3.25

319 Melopelia leucoptera
White-winged Dove .... .20 1.00 3.00

320 Columbigallina passerina terrestris
Ground Dove . ... .30 .75 2.75

320aColumbigallina passerina pallescens
Mexican Ground Dove .... .50 1.00 2.75

321 Scardafella inca
Inca Dove .... .75 1.50 3.00

[322]Geotrygon chrysia
Key West Quail-dove 2.00 5.00 7.00

[332.1]Geotrygon montana
Ruddy Quail-dove ....
[323]Starœenas cyanocephala
Blue-headed Quail-dove ....
324 Gymnogyps californianus
California Vulture $100.00 $40.00 $55.00
325 Cathartes aura
Turkey Vulture .... .50 2.50 6.00
326 Catharista urubu
Black Vulture .... .50 2.50 6.00
327 Elanoides forficatus
Swallow-tail Kite 10.00 4.00 8.00
328 Elanus leucurus
White-tailed Kite 3.00 1.50 4.50
329 Ictinia mississippiensis
Mississippi Kite 4.00 3.50 6.50
330 Rostrhamus sociabilis
Everglade Kite 10.00 6.00 10.00
331 Circus hudsonius
Marsh Hawk .... .35 1.50 4.50
332 Accipiter velox
Sharp-shinned Hawk .... 1.00 .75 3.00
333 Accipiter cooperi
Cooper's Hawk .... .30 1.00 4.00
334 Accipiter atriscapillus
American Goshawk 2.00 3.00 6.00
334a Accipiter atricapillus striatulus
Western Goshawk 3.00 3.00 6.00
335 Parabuteo unicintus harrisi
Harris's Hawk .... .50 2.00 5.00

[336] Buteo buteo
European Buzzard ....$ .35 $ 2.00 $ 5.00

337 Buteo borealis
Red-tailed Hawk .... .50 1.50 5.00

337a Buteo borealis Kriderii
Krider's Hawk 1.50 4.00 7.00

337b Buteo borealis calurus
Western Red-tail .... .50 1.50 4.00

337b Buteo borealis harlani
Harlan's Hawk 5.00 5.00 8.00

339 Buteo lineatus
Red-shouldered Hawk .... .35 1.50 4.00

339a Buteo lineatus alleni
Fla. Red-shouldered Hawk .... .50 1.75 4.00

339 Buteo lineatus elegans
Red-bellied Hawk .... .50 3.00 6.00

340 Buteo abbreviatus
Zone-tailed Hawk 3.00 4.00 7.00

341 Buteo albicaudatus sennetti
White-tailed Hawk .... .50 2.00 4.50

342 Buteo swainsoni
Swainson's Hawk .... .50 1.50 4.00

343 Buteo platypterus
Broad-winged Hawk 1.00 1.50 3.50

344 Buteo brachyurus
Short-tailed Hawk 6.00 9.00

345 Urubitinga anthracina
Mexican Black Hawk 5.00 5.00 8.00

346 Asturina plagiata
Mexican Goshawk 2.50 3.00 5.00

[347]Archibuteo lagopus
    Rough-legged Hawk ....$ .60*$ 2.00 $ 5.00
347aArchibuteo lagopus sancti-johannis
    Am. Rough-legged Hawk 2.00 2.00 5.00
348 Archibuteo ferrugineus
    Ferruginous Rough-leg 1.00 3.00 5.00
349 Aquila chrysætos
    Golden Eagle 6.00 10.00 20.00
[350]Thrasaetus harpyia
    Harpy Eagle 6.00 12.00 20.00
[351]Haliætus albicilla
    Gray Sea Eagle 2.00* 8.00 15.00
352 Haliæetus leucocephalus
    Bald Eagle 3.50 8.00 15.00
353 Falco islandus
    White Gryfalcon 5.00 15.00 20.00
354 Falco rusticolus
    Gray Gyrfalcon 6.00 15.00 20.00
354aFalco rusticolus gyrfalco
    Gyrfalcon 6.00 15.00 20.00
354bFalco rusticolus obsoletus
    Black Gyrfalcon 10.00 15.00 20.00
355 Falco mexicanus
    Prairie Falcon 2.00 2.00 5.00
356 Falco peregrinus anatum
    Duck Hawk 3.00 3.00 5.00
356aFalco peregrinus pealei
    Peale's Falcon 5.00 10.00 14.00
357 Falco columbarius
    Pigeon Hawk 2.50 1.00 3.00

357aFalco columbarius suckleyi
    Black Merlin ....$10.00 $ 3.50 $ 6.50

358 Falco richardsonii
    Richardson's Merlin 10.00 2.50 5.00

[358.1]Falco regulus
    Merlin .... .50* 1.75 4.00

359 Falco rusco cœrulessens
    Aplomado Falcon 4.00 5.00 8.00

[359.1]Falco tonnunculus
    Kestrel .... .20* 1.75 4.00

360 Falco sparverius
    American Sparrow Hawk .... .20 .60 2.50

360aFalco sparverius phalœna
    Desert Sparrow Hawk .... .20 1.00 2.75

360bFalco sparverius peninsularis ,
    St. Lucas Sparrow Hawk ....

[361]Falco dominicensis
    Cuban Sparrow Hawk............

362 Polyborus cheriway
    Audubon's Caracara 1.00 1.50 4.00

363 Polyborus lotosus
    Gaudalupe Caracara 3.00 5.00 7.00

364 Pandion haliætus carolinensis
    American Osprey .... .50 3.00 6.00

365 Strix pratincola
    American Barn Owl .... .30 3.00 5.00

366 Asio wilsonianus
    American Long-eared Owl .... .35 1.00 3.00

368 Syrnium varium
     Barred Owl ... .$ 1.00 $ 1.00 $ 3.00
368aSyrnium varium alleni
     Florida Barred Owl 1.00   1.50   3.50
369 Syrnium occidentale
     Spotted Owl 5.00   6.00 10.00
370 Scotiaptex nebulosa
     Great Gray Owl 10.00 8.00 10.00
[370a]Scotiaptex lapponica
     Lapp Owl 3.00*   8.00 12.00
371 Nyctala tengmalmi richardsoni
     Richardson's Owl 3.00   3.00   5.00
372 Nyctala acadia
     Saw-whet Owl 3.00   1.00   2.75
373 Megascops asio
     Screech Owl .... .40   1.00   2.75
373aMegascops asio floridanus
     Florida Screech Owl .... .40   1.25   3.00
373bMegascops asio trichopsis
     Texas Screech Owl .... .40   1.00   3.00
373cMegascops asio bendirei
     California Screech Owl   .... .40   1.50   3.50
373dMegascops asio kennicottii
     Kennicott's Screech Owl 1.00   2.00   4.50
373eMegascops asio maxwelliæ
     Rocky Mt. Screech Owl........... .75   2.00   3.75
373fMegascops asio cineraceus
     Mexican Screech Owl 1.50   2.00   3.50
373gMegascops asio aikeni
     Aiken's Screech Owl ....

373hMegascops asio macfarlanei
MacFarlane's Screech Owl ....
374 Megascop's flammeola
Flammulated Screech Owl ... .$ 2.75 $ 2.00 $ 4.50
374aMegascops flammeola ihahoensis
Dwarf Screech Owl ....
875 Bubo virginianus
Great Horned Owl 1.00 3.00 6.00
875aBubo virginianus subarcticus
Western Horned Owl 1.00 3.00 6.00
375bBubo virginianus arcticus
Arctic Horned Owl 5.00 6.00 10.00
375cBubo virginionus saturatus
Dusky Horned Owl 3.00 8.00 12.00
376 Nyctea nyctea
Snowy Owl 2.00* 6.00 10.00
[377]Surnia ulula
Hawk Owl 1.00* 3.00 5.00
377aSurnia ulula caparoch
Hawk Owl 1.00* 3.00 5.00
377aSurnia ulula caparoch
American Hawk Owl 3.00 3.00 5.00
378 Speotyto cunicularia hypogæa
Burrowing Owl .... .15 1.00 3.00
278aSpeotyto cunicularia floridana
Florida Burrowing Owl .... .35 3.00 5.00
379 GKlaucidium gnoma
Pygmy Owl 2.50 2.50 4.00
379aGlaucidium gnoma californicum
California Pygmy Owl 2.50 2.50 4.00
379.1Glaucidium hoskinsii
Hoskin's Pygmy Owl 10.00 12.00

380 Glaucidium phalanoides
    Ferruginous Pygmy Owl ....$ 2.25 $ 2.00 $ 4.00

381 Micropallas whitneyi
    Elf Owl 1.50   3.00   5.00

382 Conurus carolinensis
    Carolina Paroquet 10.00   5.00   7.00

[383] Crotophaga ani
    Ani 1.00   2.00   4.00

384 Crotophaga sulcirostris
    Road-runner .... .25   1.00   3.00

386 Coccyzus minor
    Mangrove Cuckoo 1.00   2.50   4.50

[386a] Coccyzus minor maynardi
    Maynard's Cuckoo 3.00   4.50

387 Coccyzus americanus
    Yellow-billed Cuckoo .... .10   .60   2.50

387a Coccyzus americanus occidentalis
    California Cuckoo .... .20   .75   2.50

388 Coccyzus erythrophthalmus
    Black-billed Cuckoo .... .10   .50   2.50

388.1 Cuculus canorus telephonus

[389] Trogon ambiguus
    Coppery-tailed Trogan 2.00   5.00   7.00

390 Ceryle alcyon
    Belted Kingfisher .... .20   .50   2.50

390.1 Ceryle torquata
    Ringed Kingfisher ....

391 Ceryle cabansi
     Texan Kingfisher .... $ 2.00 $ 1.25 $ 3.00

392 Campephilus principalis
     Ivory-billed Woodpecker 10.00   15.00   18.00

393 Dryobates villosus
     Hairy Woodpecker .... .50   .30   2.00

393aDryobates villosus leucomelus
     North. Hairy Woodpecker. .... 1.00   .30   2.00

393bDryobates villosus audubonii
     South. Hairy Woodpecker .... 1.00   .30   2.00

393cDryobates villosus harrisii
     Harris's Woodpecker .... 1.00   .75   2.50

394 Dryobates pubescens
     Downy Woodpecker .... .20   .25   1.50

394aDryobates pubescens gairdneri
     Gairdner's Woodpecker .... .50   .75   2.50

394bDryobates pubescens nomorus
     Batcheldor's Woodpecker 1.00   1.00   3.00

395 Dryobates borealis
     Red-cockaded Woodpecker .... 1.50   .50   2.00

396 Dryobates scalaris bairdii
     Baird's Woodpecker .... 1.00   .50   2.50

396aDryobates scalaris lucasanus
     Saint Lucas Woodpecker 1.50   3.00

397 Dryobates nuttallii
     Nuttall's Woodpecker 1.00   1.50   3.00

398 Dryobates arizonæ
     Arizona Woodpecker 2.00   2.00   3.00

399 Xenopicus albolarvatus
   White-headed Woodpecker ....$ 1.00 $ 1.50 $ 3.00

400 Picoides americanus
   Arctic Three-toed Woodpecker ...... 1.50   .75   2.75

401aPicoides americanus alascensis
   Alask. Three-toed Woodpecker ......

401bPicoides americanus dorsalis
   Alpine Three-toed Woodpecker 2.00   4.00

402 Sphyrapicus varius
   Yellow-bellied Sapsucker .... .25   .40   2.00

402aSphyrapicus varius nuchalis
   Red-naped Sapsucker .... 1.00   .75   2.50

403 Sphyrapicus ruber
   Red-breasted Sapsucker 1.50 1.00   2.50

404 Sphyrapicus thyroideus
   Williamson's Sapsucker 1.00 1.50   3.00

405 Ceophlœs pileatus
   Pileated Woodpecker 1.00 1.00   3.00

406 Melanerpes formicivorus bairdi
   Californian Woodpecker 40   .50   2.00

407aMelanerpes formicivorous augustifrons
   Narrow-fronted Woodpecker 1.25   2.75

408 Asyndesmus torquatus
   Lewis' Woodpecker 35 1.00   3.75

409 Centurus carolinus
   Red-bellied Woodpecker .... .10   .40   2.00

410 Centurus aurifrons
    Golden-fronted Woodpecker ....$ .50 $ .50 $ 2.00

411 Centurus uropygialis
    Gila Woodpecker 1.50 1.00 2.75

412 Colaptes auratus
    Flicker .... .05 .40 2.00

413 Colaptes cafer collaris
    Red-shafted Flicker .... .10 .50 2.00

413aColaptes cafer saturatior
    Northwestern Flicker .... .25 .60 2.00

414 Colaptes chrysoides
    Gilded Flicker .... .50 1.50 3.00

415 Colaptes rufipileus
    Gaudalupe Flicker ....

416 Antrostomus carolinensis
    Chuck-will's Widow 1.50 2.00 4.00

417 Antrostomus viciferus
    Whip-poor-will 1.00 1.00 2.50

417aAntrostomus vociferus macromystax
    Stephen's Whip-poor-will 4.00 6.00

418 Phalænoptilus nuttalli
    Poor-will 2.50 2.00 4.00

418aPhalænoptilus nuttalli nitidus
    Frosted Poor-will 3.00 2.00 4.00

418bPhalænoptilus nuttalli californicus
    Dusky Poor-will 3.00 2.00 4.00

419 Nyctidromus albicollis merrilli
    Merrill's Parauque 2.50 1.50 3.50

420 Chordeiles virginianus
    Nighthawk .... .40 .50 2.00

420aChordeiles virginianus henryi
   Western Nighthawk ....$ .40 $ .50 $ 2.00
420bChordeiles virginianus chapmani
   Florida Nighthawk 1.00   1.25   2.75
421 Chordeiles texensis
   Texas Nighthawk .... .40   .50   2.00
422 Sypseloides niger
   Black Swift 4.50   6.50
423 Chætura pelagica
   Chimney Swift 10   .50   2.00
424 Chætura vauxii
   Xaux's Swift .... .75   2.00   3.75
425 Aeronautes melanoleucus
   White-throated Swift 2.50   3.75
426 Eugenes fulgens
   Rivoli Hummingbird 3.00   4.50
427 Cœligena clemanciæ
   Blue-throated Hummingbird 3.00   4.50
428 Trochilus colubris
   Ruby-throated Hummingbird .... .50   1.00   2.00
429 Trochilus alexandri
   Black-chinned Hummingbird .... .50   1.00   2.00
430 Calypte costæ
   Costa's Hummingbird .... .75   1.00   2.00
431 Calypte anna
   Anna's Hummingbird .... .50   .75   2.00
431.1Selasphorus floresii
   Floresi's Hummingbird ....
432 Selasphorus platycercus
   Broad-tailed Hummingbird 1.00   1.25   2.50

433 Selasphorus rufus
Rufous Hummingbird . . . .$ .75 $ .75 $ 2.00

434 Selasphorus alleni
Allen's Hummingbird . . . . .75 .75 2.00

436 Stellula calliope
Calliope Hummingbird 2.00 1.25 2.50

437 Calothorax lucifer
Lucifer Hummingbird 1.50 2.50

438 Amazilis tzacatl
Reiffer's cerviniventris
Buff-bellied Hummingbird 1.50 1.00 2.00

440 Bas ilinna xantusi
Xantus's Hummingbird 3.00 4.50

440 Basilinna xantusi
White-eared Hummingbird . . . .

441 Iache latirostris
Broad-billed Hummingbird 1.50 2.50

441.1 Platypsaris albiventris
Xantus's Becard 3.00 4.50

[442] Muscivora tyrannus
Ford-tailed Flycatcher 1.50 2.50

443 Muscivora forficatus
Scissor-tailed Flycatcher . . . . .10 .60 2.00

444 Tyrannus tyrannus
Kingbird . . . . .05 .30 1.75

445 Tyrannus dominiscensis
Gray Kingbird . . . . .50 .50 2.00

446 Tyrannus melancholicus couchii
Couch's Kingbird . . . . 1.00 .75 2.00

447 Tyrannus verticalis
    Arkansas Kingbird ....$ .05 $ .45 $ 1.75
448 Tyrannus vociferans
    Cassin's Kingbird .... .25 .50 2.25
449 Pitangus derbianus
    Derby Flycatcher 1.50 3.00 4.50
[450]Myiozetetes texensis
    Giraud's Flycatcher 1.00 1.25 3.00
451 Myiodynastes luteiventris
    Sulphur-bellied Flycatcher 1.00 3.00 4.00
452 Myiarchus crinitus
    Crested Flycatcher .... .10 .30 1.50
453 Myiarchus mexicanus
    Mexican Crested Flycatcher .... .40 .30 2.00
453aMyiarchus mexicanus magister
    Arizona Crested Flycatcher 1.00 1.25 2.50
454 Myiarchus cinerascens
    Ash-throated Flycatcher .... .25 .40 1.50
454aMyiarchus cinerascens nuttingi
    Nutting's Flycatcher ....
[455]Myiarchus lawrenceii
    Lawrence's Flycatcher 1.00 2.00 3.00
455aMyiarchus lawrenceii olivascens
    Olivaceous Flycatcher 1.50 3.00
456 Sayornis phœbe
    Phœbe .... .05 .25 1.50
457 Sayornis saya
    Say's Phœbe .... .15 .35 1.50
458 Sayornis nigricans
    Black Phœbe .... .15 .50 1.75

459 Nuttalornis borealis
Olive-sided Flycatcher ....$ 1.50 $ .70 $ 2.00
460 Contopus pertinax
Cones's Flycatcher 2.00   3.50
461 Contopus virens
Wood Pewee .... .10   .25   1.50
462 Contopus richardsonii
Western Wood Pewee .... .20   .30   1.50
462aContopus richardsonii peninsulæ
Large-billed Wood Pewee ....
463 Empiodonax flavicentris
Yellow-bellied Flycatcher .... 1.00   .35   1.50
464 Empiodonax difficilis
Western Flycatcher .... .20   .35   1.50
465 Empdonax virescens
St. Lucas Flycatcher 4.00   6.00
465 Empidonax virescens
Green-crested Flycatcher .... .20   .35   1.50
466 Empiodonax traillii
Traill's Flycatcher .... .25   .60   2.00
466aEmpiodonax traillii alnorum
Alder Flycatcher .... .15   .35   1.50
467 Empiodonax minimus
Least Flycatcher .... .15   .25   1.50
468 Empidonax hammondi
Hammond's Flycatcher .... .75   .75   2.00
469 Empidonax wrightii
Wright's Flycatcher .... 1.00   .50   2.00
469.1Empidonax grieseus
Gray Flycatcher ....

[470]Empidonax fulvifrons
  Fulvous Flycatcher ... .
470aEmpidonax fulvifrons pygmæus
  Buff-breasted Flycatcher ....$ $ 2.50 $ 4.00
471 Pyroscephalus rubineus mexicanus
  Vermilion Flycatcher .... 1.00   .60   1.75
472 Ornithion imberbe
  Beardless Flycatcher .... .75   3.00   5.00
472aOrnithion imberbe ridgwayi
  Ridgway's Flycatcher 3.00   5.00
[473]Alauda arvensis
  Skylark .... .10   .60   2.00
474 Octocoris alpestris
  Horned Lark ... . 1.00   .40   1.75
474aOctocoris alpestris leucolæma
  Pallid Horned Lark .... .50   .50   2.00
474bOtocoris alpestris practicola
  Prairie Horned Lark .... .15   .50   2.00
474cOtocoris alpestris arenicola
  Desert Horned Lark .... .25   .40   2.00
474dOcocoris alpestris giraudi
  Texan Horned Lark .... .20   .50   2.00
474eOtocoris alpestris chrysolæma
  Mexican Horned Lark .... .35   .50   2.00
474fOtocoris alpestris rubæa
  Ruddy Horned Lark .... .35   .50   2.00
474gOtocoris alpestris strigata
  Streaked Horned Lark .... .75   .50   1.75
474hOtocoris alpestris adusta
  Scorched Horned Lark 1.00 1.00   3.00

474iOtocoris alpestris merrilli
Dusky Horned Lark ....$ .75 $ 1.00 $ 2.75
474jOtocoris alpestris pallida
Sonoran Horned Lark ....
475 Pica pica hudsonica
American Magpie .... .05 .75 2.50
476 Pica nuttalli
Yellow-billed Magpie .... .35 1.00 3.00
477 Cyanocitta cristata
Blue Jay .... .05 .30 1.50
477aCyanocitta cristata florincola
Florida Blue Jay .... .10 .35 1.50
478 Cyanocitta stelleri
Steller's Jay 1.00 1.75 3.00
478aCyanocitta stelleri frontalis
Blue-fronted Jay .... .75 .60 2.00
478bCyanocitta stelleri diademata
Long-crested Jay .... 1.50 .60 2.50
478cCyanocitta stelleri annectens
Black-headed Jay .... 1.50 .60 2.50
479 Aphelocoma cyanea
Florida Jay .... .75 .50 2.00
480 Aphelocoma woodhousei
Woodhouse's Jay 1.00 1.50 3.00
480.1Aphelocoma cyanotis
Blue-eared Jay ....
491 Aphelocoma californica
California Jay .... .20 .50 2.00
481aAphelocoma californica hypoleuca
Xantus's Jay ....

481bAphelocoma californica obscura
   Belding's Jay ....
481.1Apheloeoma insularis
   Santa Cruz Jay ....
482 Aphelocoma siberi arizonæ
   Arizona Jay ....$ 1.00 $ 1.00 $ 2.25
483 Xanthoura luxuosa
   Green Jay .... 1.25 .60 2.25
483 Xanthoura luxuosa
   Green Jay .... 1.25 .60 2.25
484 Perisoreus canadensis
   Canada Jay .... 1.50 .60 2.50
484aPerisoreus canadensis capitalis
   Rocky Mountain Jay 1.00 2.50
484bPerisoreus canadensis fumifrons
   Alaskan Jay 2.00 3.50
484cPerisoreus canadensis nigricapillus
   Labrador Jay 1.50 3.50
485 Perisoreus obscurus
   Oregon Jay 2.50 2.00 3.50
486 Corvus corax sinuatus
   American Raven 1.50 3.00 6.00
486aCorvus corax principalis
   Northern Raven 1.50 3.00 6.00
487 Corvus cryptoleucus
   White-necked Raven .... .50 3.00 5.50
488 Corvus americanus
   American Crow .... .05 .75 3.00
488aCorvus americanus floridanus
   Florida Crow .... .25 1.00 3.50
489 Corvus caurinus
   Northwest Crow .... .25 1.25 4.00

490 Corvus ossifragus
   Fish Crow ....$ .25 $ 1.00 $ 3.50
491 Nucifraga columbiana
   Clarke's Nutcracker 2.50   1.50   3.00
492 Cyanocephalus cyanocephalus
   Pinon Jay 50   1.00   2.50
[493]Sturnus vulgaris
   Starling 10   .50   2.00
494 Dolichonynx orzivorus
   Bobolink 25   .30   1.50
495 Molothrus ater
   Cowbird 05   .35   1.75
496 Callothrus robustus
   Bronzed Cowbird 40   .50   1.75
497 Xanthocephalus xanthocephalus
   Yellow-headed Blackbird 05   .40   1.75
498 Agelaius phœniceus
   Red-winged Blackbird 05   .25   1.50
498aAgelaius phœniceus sonoriensis
   Sonoran Red-wing 1.00   2.50
498bAgelaius phænicus bryanti
   Bahaman Red-wing 1.00   2.50
499 Agelaius gubernator
   Cicolored Blackbird 10   .45   2.00
500 Agelaius tricolor
   Tricolored Blackbird 10   .50   2.00
501 Sturnella magna
   Meadowlark 10   .50   2.00

501aSturnella magna mexicana
Mexican Meadowlark ....$ .35 $ .75 $ 2.00
501bSturnella magna neglecta
Western Meadowlark .... .10 .40 2.00
[502]Icterus icterus
Troupial 2.00 3.75
503 Icterus audubonii
Audubon's Oriole .... 2.00 .60 2.00
504 Icterus parisorum
Scott's Oriole 1.50 1.50 2.75
505 Icterus cucullatus
Hooded Oriole .... .50 .50 1.75
505aIcterus cucullatus nelsoni
Arizona Hooded Oriole .... .35 .60 1.75
506 Icterus spurius
Orchard Oriole .... .10 .35 1.75
507 Icterus galbula
Baltimore Oriole .... .10 .50 1.75
508 Icterus bullocki
Bullock's Oriole .... .10 .50 1.75
509 Scolecophagus carolinus
Rusty Blackbird .... 1.00 .40 1.75
510 Scolecophagus cyanocephalus
Brewer's Blackbird .... .05 .40 1.75
511 Quiscalus quiscula
Purple Grackle .... .05 .40 1.75
511aQuiscalus quiscula aglæus
Florida Grackle .... .10 .40 1.75
511bQuiscalus quiscula æneus
Bronzed Grackle .... .05 .40 1.75

513 Quiscalus major
    Boat-tailed Grackle ....$ .10 $ .50 $ 2.00
514 Hesperiphona vespertina
    Evening Grosbeak 1.00   1.00   2.25
514aHesperiphona vespertinus montana
    Western Evening Grosbeak 1.00   1.50   2.75
515 Pinicola enucleator
    Pine Grosbeak .... 1.25   .75   2.00
[516]Pyrrhula cassini
    Cassin's Bullfinch ....
517 Carpodacus purpureus
    Purple Finch .... .15   .25   1.50
517aCarpodacus purpureus californicus
    California Purple Finch .... .35   .40   1.75
518 Carpodacus cassini
    Cassin's Purple Finch .... 1.00   .40   1.75
519 Carpodacus mexicanus frontalis
    House Finch .... .05   .40   1.75
519bCarpodacus mexicanus ruberrimus
    St. Lucas House Finch .... .10   .40   1.75
520 Carpodacus amplus
    Guadalupe House Finch ....
521 Loxia curvirostra minor
    American Crossbill .... 5.00   .35   1.75
521aLoxia curvirostra stricklandi
    Mexican Crossbill .... 5.00   .75   2.25
522 Loxia leucoptera
    White-winged Crossbill .... 5.00   .60   2.00
523 Leucosticte griseonucha
    Aleutian Leucosticte 2.50   2.00   3.50

524 Leucosticte tephrocotis
Gray Crowned Leucosticte ....$ $ 1.00 $ 2.00

524a Leucosticte tephrocotis littoralis
Hepburn's Leucosticte 1.25 2.50

525 Leucosticte atrata
Black Leucosticte 5.00 7.00

526 Leucosticte australis
Brown-capped Leucosticte 1.00 2.50

527 Acanthis hornemannii
Greenland Redpoll 1.50 2.50 3.75

527a Acanthis hornemannii exilipes
Hoary Redpoll 1.50 2.50 3.75

528 Acanthis linaria
Redpoll .... .35* .25 1.50

528a Acanthis linaria holbœllii
Holbœll's Redpoll 2.00 3.50

528b Acanthis linaria rostrata
' Greater Redpoll 1.00 2.25

529 Astragalinus tristis
American Goldfinch .... .05 .25 1.50

529a Astragalinus tristis pallidus
Western Goldfinch .... .10 .50 1.50

530 Astragalinus psaltria
Arkansas Goldfinch .... .10 .35 1.50

530b Astragalinus psaltria mexicanus
Mexican Goldfinch .... .50 1.50 2.75

531 Astragalinus lawrencei
Lawrence's Goldfinch .... .20 .50 2.00

[532] Spinus notatus
Black-headed Goldfinch 1.25 2.50

533 Spinus pinus
  Pine Siskin ....$ 1.00 $ 1.25 $ 2.00
534 Passerina nivalis
  Snowflake .... .50*   .35   1.50
534aPasserina nivalis townsendi
  Pribilof Snowflake .... 1.50   .75   2.50
535 Passerina hyperboreus
  McKay's Snowflake 10.00   10.00
536 Calcarius lapponicus
  Lapland Longspur .... .75   .50   1.75
537 Calcarius pictus
  Smith's Longspur ... . 1.50   .50   2.00
538 Calcarius ornatus
  Chestnut-collared Longspur .... .35   .40   1.50
539 Rhynchophanes mccownii
  McCowan's Longspur .... 1.00   .40   2.00
540 Poocætes gramineus
  Vesper Sparrow .... .05   .35   ' 1.35
540aPoocætes gramineus confinis
  Western Vesper Sparrow .... .05   .35   1.50
540bPoocætes grammineus affinis
  Oregon Vesper Sparrow .... .15   .35   1.50
541 Passerculus princeps
  Ipswich Sparrow .... .25   .50   1.75
542 Passerculus sandwichensis
  Sandwich Sparrow 2.50   2.00   3.50
542aPasserculus sandwichensis savanna
  Savanna Sparrow .... .10   .25   1.50
542bPasserculus sandwichensis alaudinus
  Western Savanna Sparrow .... .20   .30   1.50

542cPasserculus sandwichensis bryanti
Bryant's Marsh Sparrow ....$ 1.00 $ 1.00 $ 2.50
543 Passerculus beldingi
Belding's Marsh Sparrow 1.00 1.50 2.75
544 Passerculus rostratus
Large-billed Sparrow 2.50 4.00
544aPasserculus rostratus guttatus
St. Lucas Sparrow 2.50 1.50 2.75
545 Coturniculus bairdii
Baird's Sparrow 1.00 2.50
546 oturniculus savannarum passerinus
Grasshopper Sparrow .... .20 .30 1.50
546aCoturniculus savannarum bimaculatus
West. Grasshopper Sparrow .... .20 .35 1.50
547 Coturniculus henslowii
Henslow's Sparrow .... 1.50 .75 2.00
547aCoturniculus henslowii occidentalis
Western Henslow's Sparrow ....
548 Coturniculus leconteii
Leconte's Sparrow .... .60 2.00
549 Ammodramus caudacutus
Sharp-tailed Sparrow .... .35 .35 1.50
549aAmmodramus caudacutus nelsoni
Nelson's Sparrow .... .60 2.25
549bAmmodramus caudacutus subvirgatus
Acadian Sharp-tailed Sparrow ...... .35 2.00
550 Ammodramus maritimus
Seaside Sparrow .... .20 .40 1.50
550aAmmodramus maritimus peninsulæ
Scott's Seaside Sparrow 1.25 2.50

550b Ammodramus maritimus sennetti			
Texan Seaside Sparrow ....$	$ 2.00	$	3.50
551 Ammodramus nigrescens			
Dusky Seaside Sparrow		1.25	2.50
552 Chondestes grammacus			
Lark Sparrow	.05	.40	1.75
552a Chondestes grammacus strigatus			
Western Lark Sparrow	.05	.30	1.50
553 Zonotrichia querula			
Harris's Sparrow		.50	2.00
554 Zonotrichia leucophrys			
White-crowned Sparrow	.50	.35	1.50
554a Zonotrichia leucophyrs intermedia			
Intermediate Sparrow	1.00	.35	1.75
554b Zonotrichia leucophrys gambeli			
Gambell's Sparrow	.15	.35	1.50
557 Zonotrichia coronata			
Golden-crowned Sparrow	1.50	.50	2.00
558 Zonotrichia albicollis			
White throated Sparrow	.35	.25	1.50
559 Spizella monticola			
Tree Sparrow	.75	.25	1.50
559a Spizella monticola ochracea			
Western Tree Sparrow	.75	.35	1.50
560 Spizella socialis			
Chipping Sparrow	.05	.25	1.25
560a Spizella socialis arizonæ			
Western Chipping Sparrow	.10	.30	1.50
561 Spizella pallida			
Clay colored Sparrow	.35	.30	1.75

562 Spizella breweri
    Brewer's Sparrow ... .$ .35 $ .40 $ 1.75
563 Spizella pusilla
    Field Sparrow 05   .25   1.25
563aSpizella pusilla arenacea
    Western Field Sparrow 25   .75   2.00
564 Spizella wortheni
    Worthen's Sparrow 2.00   3.50
565 Spizella atrigularis
    Black chinned Sparrow 1.00   2.00   3.50
566 Junco aikeni
    White-winged Junco .... 1.50   .75   2.50
567 Junco hyemalis
    Slate-colored Junco 20   .25   1.50
567aJunco hyemalis oregonus
    Oregon Junco 50   .50   1.75
567bJunco hyemalis shufeldti
    Shufeldt's Junco 75   2.00   3.75
567cJunco hyemalis thurberi
    Thurber's Junco 75   2.00   3.75
567dJunco hyemalis pinosus
    Point Jinos Junco ....
567eJunco hyemalis carolinensis
    Carolina Junco 60   1.00   2.50
568 Junco annectens
    Pink-sided Junco .... 1.50   .50   2.00
568.1Junco ridgwayi
    Ridgway's Junco .. ..
569 Junco caniceps
    Gray-headed Junco .... 1.00   .60   2.00

570 Junco phæonotus palliatus
    Arizona Junco ....$ 1.00 $ .60 $ 2.00
570aJunco phæonotus dorsalis
    Red-backed Junco .... 1.00   .60   2.00
571 Junco bairdi
    Baird's Junco 3.00   4.50
571.1Junco townsendi
    Townsend's Junco ....
572 Junco insularis
    Guadalupe Junco ....
573 Amphispiza bileneata
    Black-throated Sparrow .... .35   .50   1.75
574 Amphispiza belli
    Bell's Sparrow .... .75   .50   1.75
574aAmphispiza belli nevadensis
    Sage Sparrow 1.00   1.00   2.50
574bAmphispiza belli cinerea
    Cinereous Sparrow 1.00   1.00   2.50
575 Peucæa æstivalis
    Pine-wood Sparrow 1.00   1.00   2.50
575aPeucæa æstivalis bachmanii
    Bachman's Sparrow 1.50   1.00   2.50
576 Peucæa botteri
    Arizona Sparrow 2.00   1.00   2.50
578 Peucæa cassini
    Cassin's Sparrow .... 1.50   .75   1.50
579 Aimophila carpalis
    Rufous-winged Sparrow 375   1.00   3.75
580 Aimophila ruficeps
    Rufous-crowned Sparrow .... 2.00   .75   2.25

580aAimophila ruficeps boucardi
    Boucard's Sparrow ....$ 2.00 $ 1.00 $ 2.50
580bAimophila ruficeps eremœca
    Rock Sparrow 2.00   1.00   2.50
581 Melospiza cinerea melodia
    Song Sparrow 15   .25   1.50
581aMelospiza cinerea fallax
    Desert Song Sparrow 35   .35   1.50
581bMelospiza cinerea montana
    Mountain Song Sparrow 25   .35   2.00
581cMelospiza cinerea heermanni
    Heermann's Song Sparrow 10   .35   2.00
581dMelospiza cinerea samuelis
    Samuel's Song Sparrow 05   .30   1.50
581eMelospiza cinerea guttata
    Rusty Song Sparrow 40   .50   2.00
581fMelospiza cinerea rufina
    Sooty Song Sparrow 50   1.00   2.50
581gMelospiza cinerea rivularis
    Brown's Song Sparrow ....
581hMelospiza cinerea graminea
    Santa Barbara Song Sparrow ....
581i Melospiza cinerea clementæ
    San Clemente Song Sparrow .....
581.1Melospizo insignis
    Bischoff's Song Sparrow ....
582 Melospiza cinerea
    Aleutian Song Sparrow 3.00   5.00   7.00
583 Melospiza lincolni
    Lincoln's Sparrow 75   .30   1.75

583aMelospiza lincolni striata
Forbush's Sparrow ....
584 Melospiza georgiana
Swamp Sparrow ....$ .10 $ .30 $ 1.50
585 Passerella ilaca
Fox Sparrow .... 1.00 .25 1.50
585aPasserella iliaca unalaschcensis
Townsend's Sparrow .... 2.00 .40 2.00
585bPasserella ilaca megarhyncha
Thick-billed Sparrow .... 2.00 .50 2.00
585cPasserella iliaca schistacea
Slate-colored Sparrow 2.00 2.00 3.00
586 Arremenops rufivirgata
Texas Sparrow .... .50 .50 2.00
587 Pipilo erythropthalmus
Towhee .... .10 .25 1.75
587aPipilo erythrophthalmus alleni
White-eyed Towhee .... .50 .40 2.00
588 Pipilo maculatus arcticus
Arctic Towhee .... .75 .40 2.00
588aPipilo maculatus megalonyx
Spurred Towhee .... .20 .40 2.00
588bPipilo maculatus oregonus
Oregon Towhee .... .25 .40 2.00
589 Pipilo consobrinus
Guadalupe Towhee ....
590 Oreospiza chlorura
Green tailed Towhee .... .50 .50 2.00
591 Pipilo fuscus mesoleucus
Canon Towhee .... .50 .40 1.75

591a Pipilo fuscus albigula
  St. Lucas Towhee ....$ 1.00 $ 2.00 $ 3.00
591b Pipilo fuscus crissalis
  California Towhee ....   .10.   .40   2.00
591c Pipilo fuscus senicula
  Anthony's Towhee ....
592 Pipilo aberti
  Abert's Towhee 75   1.25   2.75
593 Cardinalis cardinalis
  Cardinal 05   .30   1.75
593a Cardinalis cardinalis superbus
  Arizona Cardinal 10   .65   2.00
593b Cardinalis cardinalis igneus
  St. Lucas Cardinal 1.50   1.00   2.50
953c Cardinalis cardinalis canicaudus
  Gray-tailed Cardinal 75   2.25
594 Pyrrhuloxia sinuata
  Texan Cardinal 35   1.00   2.50
594a Pyrrhuloxia sinuata texana
  Arizona Pyrrhuloxia 2.00   1.00   2.00
594b Pyrrhuloxia sinuata peninsulæ
  St. Lucas Pyrrhuloxia ··········1 50   I 00   2 50
595 Zamelodia ludoviciana
  Rose-breasted Grosbeak 10   .45   1.75
596 Habia melanocephala
  Black-headed Grosbeak ·········· 15   50   2.00
597 Guiraca cærulea
  Blue Grosbeak 20   .60   2.00 ·
597a Guiraca cærulea lazula
  Western Blue Grosbeak 20   .60   2.00

598 Cyanospiza cyanea
    Indigo Bunting ....$ .10 $ .30 $ 1.50
599 Cyanospiza amœna
    Lazuli Bunting .... .20 .50 2.00
600 Cyanospiza versicolor
    Varied Bunting 1.50 2.75
600aCyanospiza versicolor pulchra
    Beautiful Bunting 7.00 8.50
601 Cyanospiza ciris
    Painted Bunting .... .10 .60 1.75
602 Sporophila morelleti sharpei
    Sharpe's Seed-eater .... .50 .60 2.00
603 Tiaris bicolor
    Grassquit 1.00 1.00 2.25
[603.1]Tiaris canora
    Melodious Grassquit ....
604 Spiza americana
    Dickcissel .... .05 .30 1.75
605 Calamospiza melanocorys
    Lark Bunting .... .25 .40 2.00
606 Euphonia elegantissima
    Blue-headed Euphonia 2.00 1.25 2.75
607 Piranga ludoviciana
    Louisiana Tanager .... .75 .75 2.00
608 Piranga erythromelas
    Scarlet Tanager .... .25 .60 2.00
609 Piranga hepatica
    Hepatica Tanager 1.50 1.50 3.00
610 Piranga rubra
    Summer Tanager .... .25 .60 2.00

610aPiranga rubra cooperi
   Coopers Tanager ....$ 1.50 $ 1.50 $ 3.00
611 Urogne subis
   Purple Martin 10   .40   2.00
611aProgne subis hesperia
   Western Martin 60   2.00
611.1Progne crptoleuca
   Cuban Martin 1.25   3.00
612 Petrochelidon lunifrons
   Cliff Swallow 05   .30   1.75
[612.1]Petrochelidon fulva
   Cuban Cliff Swallow ....
613 Hirundo erythrogastra
   Barn Swallow 05   .30   1.75
614 Tachycineta bicolor
   Tree Swallow 15   .30   1.75
615 Tacycineta thalassina
   Violet-green Swallow 40   .60   2.00
[615.1]Callichelidon cyaneoviridis
   Bahamian Swallow ....
616 Riparia riparia
   Bank Swallow 05   .25   1.50
617 Stelgidopteryx serripennis
   Rough-winged Swallow 25   .50   2.00
618 Ampelis garrulus
   Bohemian Waxwing 1.50   1.25   2.75
619 Ampelis cedrorum
   Cedar Waxwing 10   .25   1.75
620 Phainopepla nitens
   Phainopepla 30   .90   2.50

621 Lanius borealis
    Northern Shrike ....$ 1.00 $ .50 $ 2.00
622 Lanius ludovicianus
    Loggerhead Shrike .... .05   .40   2.00
622aLanius ludovicianus excubitorides
    White-rumped Shrike .... .05   .30   2.00
622bLanius ludovicianus gambeli
    California Shrike .... .05   .30   2.00
623 Vireo calidris barbatulus
    Black-whiskered Vireo .... 1.50   .75   2.50
624 Vireo olivaceus
    Red-eyed Vireo .... .10   .25   1.75
625 Vireo flavoviridis
    Yellow-green Vireo 1.50   1.25   2.75
626 Vireo philadelphicus
    Philadelphia Vireo 60   2.00
627 Vireo gilvus
    Warbling Vireo .... .15   .25   1.75
628 Vireo flavifrons
    Yellow-throated Vireo .... .25   .30   1.75
629 Vireo solitarius
    Blue-headed Vireo .... 1.00   .35   1.75
629aVireo solitarius cassinii
    Cassin's Vireo .... 1.00   .60   2.00
629bVireo solitarius plumbeus
    Plumbeous Vireo .... .75   .50   2.00
629cVireo solitarius alticola
    Mountain Solitary Vireo .... .75   .50   2.00
629dVireo solitarius lucasanus
    St. Lucas Solitary Vireo 1.00   2.50

630 Vireo atricapillus
  Black-capped Vireo ....$ 1.00 $ 1.00 $ 2.50
631 Vireo noveboracensis
  White-eyed Vireo 15   .30   1.50
631aVireo noveboracensis maynardi
  Key West Vireo 1.50   1.50   3.00
632 Vireo huttoni
  Hutton's Vireo ....   2.00   .60   2.00
632aVireo huttoni stephensi
  Stephen's Vireo ....   2.00   .75   2.00
632cVireo huttoni obscurus
  Anthony's Vireo ....
633 Vireo Bellii
  Bell's Vireo 10   .50   1.75
633aVireo bellii pusillus
  Least Vireo 75   1.00   2.50
634 Vireo vicinior
  Gray Vireo 1.50   1.00   2.50
635 Cœreba bahamensis
  Bahama Honey Creeper 1.25   2.00   3.25
636 Mniotilta varia
  Black and White Warbler 50   .35   1.50
637 Protonotaria citrea
  Prothonotary Warbler 25   .75   2.25
638 Helinaia swainsonii
  Swainson's Warbler 1.00   2.50   4.00
639 Helmitheros vermivorus
  Worm-eating Warbler 75   .75   2.25
640 Helminthophila bachmani
  Bachman's Warbler 3.00   4.50

292   Guide to Taxidermy

641 Helminthophila pinus
    Blue-winged Teal ....$ 1.50 $ .75 $ 2.25
642 Helminthophila chrysoptera
    Golden-winged Warbler .... .75   .60   2.00
643 Helminthophila luciæ
    Lucy's Warbler 2.00   1.50   2.75
644 Helminthophila virginiæ
    Virginia's Warbler 2.50   2.50   3.75
645 Helminthophila rubricapilla
    Nashville Warbler .... .75   .30   1.75
645aHelminthophila rubricapilla gutturalis
    Calaveras Warbler 35   2.00
646 Helminthophila celata
    Orange-crowned Warbler .... 2.00   .60   2.00
646aHelminthophila celata lutescens
    Lutescent Warbler .... .75   .60   2.25
646bHelminthophila celata sordida
    Dusky Warbler ....
647 Helminthophila peregrina
    Tennessee Warbler 1.00   2.50
648 Compsothlypis americana
    Parula Warbler .... .20   .25   1.50
649 Compsothlypis nigrilora
    Sennett's Warbler .... 2.00   .75   2.50
650 Dendroica tigrina
    Cape May Warbler 1.25   2.50
651 Dendroica olivacea
    Olive Warbler 5.00   2.50   4.00
652 Dendroica æstiva
    Yellow Warbler .... .05   .30   1.50

652aDendroica æstiva sonorana
Sonora Yellow Warbler ....$ .50 $ .50 $ 2.00
653 Dendroica bryanto castaneiceps
Mangrove Warbler 8.00 10.00
654 Dendroica cærulescens
Black-throated Blue Warbler......... 1.25 .35 1.75
655 Dendroica coronata
Myrtle Warbler .... .75 .25 1.75
656 Dendroica auduboni
Audubon's Warbler .... 1.50 .50 2.00
657 Dendroica maculosa
Magnolia Warbler .... .50 .30 1.75
658 Dendroica cærulea
Cerulean Warbler .... 1.75 .75 2.00
659 Dendroica pensylvanica
Chestnut-sided Warbler .... .15 .25 1.75
660 Dendroica castanea
Bay-breasted Warbler .... 1.50 .75 2.25
661 Dendroica striata
Black-poll Warbler .... .75 .25 1.50
662 Dendroica blackburniæ
Blackburnian Warbler .... 2.00 .50 2.00
663 Dendroica dominica
Yellow-throated Warbler .... 1.50 .60 2.00
663aDendroica dominica albilora
Sycamore Warbler .... 2.00 .65 2.00
664 Dendroica graciæ
Grace's Warbler 2.50 3.00 4.50
665 Dendroica nigrescens
Black-throated Gray Warbler 2.50 1.00 2.50

666 Dendroica chrysoparia
   Golden cheeked Warbler ....$ 2.00 $ 6.00 $ 8.00
667 Dendroica virens
   Black throated Green Warbler 50   .30   1.75
668 Dendroica townsendi
   Townsend's Warbler 2.00   2.50   4.00
669 Dendroica occidentalis
   Hermit Warbler 5.00   2.50   4.00
670 Dendroica kirtlandi
   Kirtland's Warbler 6.00   7.50
671 Dendroica vigorsii
   Pine Warbler 50   .30   1.75
672 Dendroica palmarum
   Palm Warbler ....   3.00   .50   1.75
672aDendroica palmarum hyprochrysea
   Yellow Palm Warbler 25   1.75
673 Dendroica discolor
   Prairie Warbler 30   .40   1.75
674 Seiurus aurocapillus
   Oven bird 20   .25   1.75
675 Seiurus noveboracensis
   Water-Thrush 50   .30   1.75
675aSeiurus noveboracensis notabillis
   Grinnell's Water-Thrush .... 1.50   .75   2.25
676 Seiurus motacilla
   Louisiana Water-Thrush 50   .75   2.25
677 Geothlypis formosa
   Kentucky Warbler 75   1.00   2.00
678 Geothlypis agilis
   Connecticut Warbler 1.00   1.00   2.50

679 Geothlypis philadelphia
    Mourning Warbler ....$ 2.50 $ .75 $ 2.50

680 Geothlypis macgillivrayi
    Macgillivray's Warbler .... 1.50   .75   2.25

681 Geothlypis trichas
    Maryland Yellow-throat .... .20   .25   1.50

681aGeothlypis trichas occidentalis
    Western Yellow-throat .... .25   .50   1.75

681bGeothlypis trichas ignota
    Florida Yellow-throat 1.00   1.00   2.25

682 Geothlypis beldingi
    Belding's Yellow-throat 4.00   5.50

682.1Geothlypis poliocephala ralphi
    Rio Grande Yellow-throat 2.00   3.50

683 Icteria virens
    Yellow-breasted Chat .... .10   .40   1.75

683aIcteria virens longicauda
    Long-tailed Chat .... .10   .40   1.75

684 Wilsonia mitrata
    Hooded Warbler .... .50   .60   2.00

685 Wilsonia pusilla
    Wilson's Warbler .... 1.00   .50   1.75

685aWilsonia pusilla pileolata
    Pileoated Warbler .... .75   .50   2.00

686 Wilsonia canadensis
    Canadian Warbler .. .. 1.50   .40   1.75

687 Setophaga ruticilla
    American Redstart .... .15   .25   1.50

688 Setophaga picta
    Painted Redstart 2.00   2.00   3.50

[689]Setophaga miniata
   Red-bellied Redstart ....$ $ 2.50 $ 4.00
690 Cardellina rubrifrons
   Red-faced Warbler 2.50   2.00   3.50
[691]Ergaticus ruber
   Red Warbler 3.00   4.50
[692]Basileuterus culcivorus
   Brasher's Warbler 3.00   4.50
[692]Basileuterus culicivorus
   Bell's Warbler 3.00   4.50
[694]Motacilla alba
   White Wagtail .... .10*   .65   2.00
[695]Motacilla ocularis
   Swinhoe's Wagtail ....
696 Budytes flavus leucostriatus
   Siberian Yellow Wag-tail .... 1.00   .75   2.25
697 Anthus pensilvanicus
   American Pipit .... .75   .30   1.75
[698]Anthus pratensis
   Meadow Pipit   .... .10*   .60   2.00
[699]Anthus cervinus
   Red-throated Pipit .... .75*   2.00   3.25
700 Anthus spragueii
   Sprague's Pipit 3.00   1.50   3.00
701 Cinclus mexicanus
   American Dipper .... 1.00   .75   2.25
702 Oroscoptes montanus
   Sage Thrasher ....,........ .50   .50   2.00
703 Mimus polyglottos
   Mockingbird .... .05   .50   2.00

704 Galeoscoptes carolinensis
Catbird ....$ .05 $ .35 $ 2.00

705 Toxostoma rufum
Brown Thrasher .... .05 .40 2.00

706 Toxostoma longirostre sennetti
Sennett's Thrasher .... .15 .40 2.00

707 Toxostoma curvirostre
Curve-billed Thrasher .... .15 .40 2.00

707a Toxostoma curvirostre palmeri
Palmer's Thrasher .... .75 1.00 3.00

708 Toxostoma bendirei
Bendire's Thrasher .... .75 1.00 3.00

709 Toxostoma cinereum
St. Lucas Thrasher 3.00 1.50 3.00

709a Toxostoma cinereus mearnsi
Mearn's Thrasher ....

710 Toxostoma redivivum
California Thrasher .... .20 .75 2.50

711 Toxostoma lecontei
Leconte's Thrasher 2.00 2.00 3.75

712 Toxostima crissalis
Crissal Thrasher 1.00 2.00 3.50

713 Heleodytes brunneicapillus
Cactus Wren ... . .10 .75 2.25

713a Helodytes brunneicapillus bryanti
Bryant's Cactus Wren ....

715 Salpinctes obsoletus
Rock Wren .... .50 .50 2.00

716 Salpinctes guadeloupensis
Guadalupe Rock Wren ....

[717]Catherpes mexicanus
   White-throated Wren ....$ .75 $ 1.25 $ 2.50
717aCatherpes mexicanus conspersus
   Canon Wren 60   1.25   2.50
717bCatherpes mexicanus punctulatus
   Dotted Canon Wren 1.25   2.50
718 Thryothorus ludovicianus
   Carolina Wren 10   .40   1.75
718aThryothorus ludovicianus miamensis
   Florida Wren 50   1.00   2.25
718bThryothorus ludovicianus lomitensis
   Lomita Wren 75   2.00   3.50
719 Thryothorus bewickii
   Bewick's Wren 25   .75   2.00
719aThryothorus bewickii spilurus
   Vigor's Wren 25   .75   2.00
719bThryothorus bewickii bairdi
   Baird's Wren 25   .75   2.00
719.1Thryothorus leucophrys
   San Clemante Wren ....
720 Thryothorus brevicaudus
   Guadalupe Wren ....
721 Troglodytes aedon
   House Wren 05   .30   .75
721aTroglodytes aedon parkmanii
   Parkman's Wren 10   .35   .75
721bTroglodytes aedon aztecus
   Western House Wren 10   .35   .75
722 Troglodytes hiemalis
   Winter Wren ....   1.00   .40   1.75

722aTroglodytes hiemalis pacificus
Western Winter Wren ....$ 1.00 $ .50 $ 2.00

723 Troglodytes alascensis
Alaskan Wren 3.00 4.50

724 Cistothorus stellaris
Short-billed Marsh Wren .... 1.00 .75 2.25

725 Cistothorus palustris
Long-billed Marsh Wren .... .05 .25 1.75

725aCistothorus palustris paludicola
Tule Wren . ... .10 .40 1.75

725cCistothorus palustris griseus
Worthington's Marsh Wren ....

725.1Cistothorus marianæ
Marian's Marsh Wren .... .40 2.25

726 Certhia familiaris americana
Brown Creeper .... .75 .30 1.75

726aCerthia familiaris atticola
Mexican Creeper .... 1.50 .75 2.00

726bCerthia familiaris montana
Rocky Mountain Creeper .... 1.50 .45 2.00

726cCerthia familiaris occidentalis
California Creeper .... 1.25 .45 1.75

727 Sitta Carolinensis
White-breasted Nuthatch .... .35 .30 1.75

727aSitta carolinensis aculeata
Slender-billed Nuthatch .... .75 .40 2.00

727bSitta carolinensies atkinsi
Fla. White-breasted Nuthatch .... .50 1.00 2.00

728 Sitta canadensis
Red-breasted Nuthatch .... 1.00 .35 1.75

729 Sitta pusilla
    Brown-headed Nuthatch ....✳ .25 ✳ .35 $ 1.75
730 Sitta pygmæa
    Pygmy Nuthatch .... .50   .35   1.75
730aSitta pygmæa leuconucha
    White-naped Nuthatch ....
731 Bæolophus bicolor
    Tufted Titmouse .... .35   .35   1.75
731aBæolophus bicolor texensis
    Texan Tufted Titmouse .... .75   .35   1.75
732 Bæolophus atricristatus
    Black-crested Titmouse .... .75   .40   2.00
733 Bæolophus inoratus
    Plain Titmouse 50   .50   2.00
733aBæolophus inoratus griseus
    Gray Titmouse 75   2.25
733bBæolophus inoratus cineraceus
    Ashy Titmouse 1.00   2.50
734 Bæolophus wollwerberi
    Bridled Titmouse .... 2.00   .75   2.25
735 Parus atricapillus
    Chickadee .... .10   .25   1.50
735aParus atricapillus sententrionalis
    Long-tailed Chickadee .... .50   .60   1.75
735bParus atricapillus occidentalis
    Oregon Chickadee .... .35   .65   1.75
736 Parus carolinensis
    Carolina Chickadee .... .15   .35   1.75
736aParus carolinensis agilis
    Plubeous Chickadee .... .50   1.00   2.50

737 Parus meridionalis
     Mexican Chickadee ....$ $ 2.00 $ 3.25
738 Parus gambeli
     Mountain Chickadee .... 1.00   .75   2.00
739 Parus cinctus obtectus
     Siberian Chickadee 2.50   5.00   6.50
740 Parus hudsonicus
     Hudsonian Chickadee .... 1.25   .40   1.75
740aParus hudsonicus stoneyi
     Kowak Chickadee 80   2.25
740bParus hudsonicus columbianus
     Columbian Chickadee ....
741 Parus rufescens
     Chestnut-backed Chickadee .... .75   1.00   2.25
741aParus rufescens neglectus
     Californian Chickadee .... .50   .65   2.00
742 Chamæa fasciata
     Wren-Tit 50   .60   2.00
742aChamæa fasciata henshawi
     Pallid Wren-Tit .... .75   1.25   2.50
743 Psaltriparus minimus
     Bush-Tit 25   .35   1.75
743aPsaltriparus minimus californicus
     California Bush-Tit .... .15   .35   1.75
743bPsaltriparus minimus grindæ
     Grinda's Bush-Tit 1.50   3.00
744 Psaltriparus plumbeus
     Lead-colored Bush-Tit .... 1.50   .30   1.75
744.1Psaltriparus santaritæ
     Santa Rica Bush-Tit 1.50   2.75

745 Psaltriparus lloydi			
Lloyd's Bush-Tit ....$		$ 1.25	$ 2.50
746 Auriparus flaviceps			
Verdin	.75	.50	1.75
747 Phyllopseutstes borealis			
Kennicott's Willow Warbler	2.00	5.00	7.00
748 Regulus satrapa			
Golden-crowned Kinglet	1.00	.30	1.7*
748aRegulus satrapa olivaceus			
W. Golden-crowned Kinglet	1.00	.40	1.75
749 Regulus calendula			
Ruby-crowned Kinglet	2.00	.45	1.75
750 Regulus obscurus			
Dusky Kinglet	1.50	.75	2.00
751 Polioptila cærulea			
Blue-gray Gnatcatcher	.30	.30	1.75
751aPolioptila cværulea obscura			
Western Gnatcatcher	.50	.65	2.00
752 Polioptila plumbea			
Plumbeus Gnatcatcher	.75	.75	2.00
753 Polioptila californica			
Black-tailed Gnatcatcher	.50	.50	2.00
754 Myadestes townsendii			
Townsend's Solitaire	1.00	.40	2.00
755 Hylocichla mustelinus			
Wood Thrush	.05	.30	1.75
756 Hylocichla fuscescens			
Wilson's Thrush	.10	.30	1.50
756aHylocichla fuscencens salicicola			
Willow Thrush	1.00	.75	2.25

757 Hylocichla aliciæ
   Gray-cheeked Thrush ....$ .50 $ .35 $ 2.00
757aHylocichla aliciæa bicknelli
   Bicknell's Thrush 75   2.25
758 Hylocichla ustulatus
   Russet-backed Thrush 15   .45   2.00
758aHylocichla ustulatus swainsonii
   Olive-backed Thrush 35   .30   1.75
759 Hylocichla guttata
   Dwarf Hermit Thrush .... 1.50   .40   2.00
759aHylocichla guttata auduboni
   Audubon's Hermit Thrush .... 1.00   .40   2.00
759bTylocichla guttata pallasii
   Hermit Thrush 30   .35   1.75
[760]Turdus iliacus
   Red-winged Thrush ....   .25*   .75   2.25
761 Merula migratoria
   American Robin 03   .30   1.75
761aMerula migratoria propinqua
   Western Robin 10   .50   2.00
762 Merula confinis
   St. Lucas Robin 4.00   5.25
763 Ixoreus naevius
   Varied Thrush .... 2.50   .75   2.25
[764]Cyanecula suecica
   Red-spotted Bluethroat 75* 1.25   2.75
765 Saxicola œnanthe
   Wheatear ....   .10*   .50   2.00
766 Sialia sialis
   Bluebird 05   .25   1.75

INDEX